LIVE | DEAD

THE JOURNEY

AN INTERACTIVE PRAYER ADVENTURE FOR UNREACHED PEOPLE GROUPS

WRITTEN BY MISSIONARIES WHO LOVE THE ARAB WORLD

Compiled and Edited by Dick Brogden, Mike Murray, Charity Reeb & Mark Renfroe

ISBN: 978-1-93783-093-9
Printed in the United States of America
16 15 14 13 • 2 3 4 5 6

OUT OF 100,000 MISSIONARIES SERVING AROUND THE WORLD,
ABOUT 3% WORK AMONG UNREACHED PEOPLE GROUPS.

THIS BOOK IS DEDICATED TO THE 3%
IN HOPES THAT THIS NUMBER WILL RISE.

CONTENTS

INTRODUCTION

What Is Live Dead?   6

What Should I Expect on My Journey?   12

Basics of Islam   14

Intercede   15

Kingdom Prayers   16

FAITH JOURNEYS

STOP 1   A Walk Through Cairo   18

STOP 2   The Value of Abiding   26

STOP 3   A Walk Through Damascus   48

STOP 4   The Value of Community   54

STOP 5   The Role of the Holy Spirit as Guide   76

STOP 6   A Walk Through Doha   80

STOP 7   The Value of Partnering   88

STOP 8   A Walk Through Muscat   112

STOP 9   The Value of Team   118

STOP 10   The Role of the Holy Spirit in Maintaining a Soft Heart in Hard Places   142

STOP 11   The Value of Apostolic Function   146

STOP 12   The Value of Transformation   170

STOP 13   A Walk Through Benghazi   188

STOP 14   The Value of Sacrifice   194

STOP 15   Reflection: When Daddy Goes to Prison   208

STOP 16   The Value of Character   216

STOP 17   The Value of Lifelong Learning   240

STOP 18   A Walk Through Jeddah   256

STOP 19   The Role of the Holy Spirit in Maintaining a Soft Heart in Hard Times   262

STOP 20   The Value of Accountability   266

STOP 21   A Walk Through Tunis   288

STOP 22   The Value of Pioneering   294

STOP 23   Living and Dying Daily for the Pleasure of the One   312

CONCLUSION   316

ENDNOTES   318

SUGGESTED READING   320

ABOUT THE COLLABORATORS   322

WHAT IS LIVE DEAD?

BY DICK BROGDEN & MARK RENFROE

In one sense, Live Dead is timeless and universal. It is the crucified life, the "I die daily" of Paul, the death to self that unbroken generations of Christ followers from all cultures have faithfully lived. All who bear the name of Jesus are called to put His passions and priorities above their own needs and comforts. We all are to live dead.

In another sense, Live Dead is a very intentional effort to preach the gospel of the Kingdom among every nation that the end may come (Matthew 24:14). Following the 1800s, the great century of Christian mission, came the realization that our world is not getting better, and that peace and justice cannot be ultimately realized by the efforts of man—including redeemed man. A longing, a desperation for Christ to return, filled the hearts of believers in Jesus as the twentieth century dawned.

Desperate for Jesus to come back, understanding that His return was linked to the gospel being preached to every people (to every ethnolinguistic group), aware that this could not be done in their own power, believers from around the world got on their knees and pleaded for power from on high.

One hundred years later we still pray, as William Carey suggested, with open Bible and open map, and see that there are yet 6,000-plus people groups who are unreached with the gospel. Forty percent of our world does not have a Christian friend.

Live Dead, in the specific sense then, is an effort to see Jesus glorified by every ethnolinguistic people on earth that the Scripture may be fulfilled and our King of Kings return to rule and reign forever. Jesus called us to make disciples of all peoples, and we are convinced that the best means to do this is by planting churches. This is the nonnegotiable core of Live Dead: church planting, unreached peoples, and team.

The reality is that many of the peoples who remain to be reached are found in contexts of oppression, war, restricted access, instability, poverty, and inhospitable climates. Some combination of manic ideology, spiritual oppression, political chaos, intemperate living conditions, unavailable schooling or health care, etc., makes these peoples very difficult to live among. If we are going to reach them (by planting churches among them through teams), there is going to be a cost. It will not be easy. It will take blood and boldness, sweat and suffering, tears and tenacity. Some will be imprisoned, some will die, some will spend a lifetime of labor with little credit and little reward. All will have to live dead in one manner or another.

Missions in our era does not restrict the unreached to the rural poor. While it is true that many Muslim unreached people groups live in hard-to-reach and inhospitable places like Yemen and Libya, some of the most unreached Arabs live in wealthy, modern urban centers like Doha, the capital of Qatar, one of the richest nations on earth. If we only see people who are poorer than us as needy, it is implied arrogance. What if the wealthy don't need our water wells? Our pride can keep us away from those who look down upon us; our hubris and insecurity sometimes lead us to work among those for whom we can provide. Everybody likes to be a savior. The challenge of the wealthy, urban, unreached Muslim in the Arabian Gulf is often two-edged: Not only does Islam bind them, but they also need absolutely nothing practical from us. We are forced to preach the gospel in utter weakness.

To live dead is to journey. It is not momentary heroism or occasional folly; it is a life dedicated to following Jesus—no matter the cost. We are not the first to embark on this journey; we follow in the footsteps of Paul, the Celts, Franciscans, Moravians, Carey, Taylor, Elliot, Townsend, McGavran, Winter, and thousands of colleagues from the Global South. No, we are not the first, but we very well could be the last. If we are joyfully willing to pay any price (to live or die) that Jesus be glorified by every people everywhere. Then the end shall come.

LIVE DEAD IN THE ARAB CONTEXT

The Sudanese have a poignant proverb: "If you want to kill an elephant, you cannot stab its shadow." Jesus taught a similar truth when He observed that if you want to plunder the strong man's house, you first have to bind the strong man. The premier challenge to the gospel in our age is Islam. The heart of Islam is the Arab world. The financial center (petro-dollars), the emotional center (Mecca), and the ideological center (Cairo) all are found in the Arab world. Yes, there are countries with more Muslims in them than Saudi Arabia or Egypt, but if there was a massive revival among Saudi Arabians, it would have more impact on the world of Islam (and beyond) than a similar revival in any other Muslim country.

If we truly want to see the gospel preached in all the world among every people, we must make a concentrated effort to preach among Muslims. And again, the Muslim center is the Arab world.

European powers in the eighteenth and nineteenth centuries squabbled over access to the Middle East. Trade routes and resources drove France, England, and Russia to intervene and ultimately to colonize the Arab world. Post-World War II bankruptcy led to independence and euphoria among Arab Muslims. This euphoria was short lived as totalitarian governments, selfish monarchies, or despotic dictators replaced colonial masters.

In 2011, revolutions spread across the Arab world. These successive revolts (which started in Tunisia and spread to Libya, Egypt, Yemen, Syria, and beyond) came to be known as the Arab Spring. Arabs, Muslim, and Christian, rose up to throw off oppressive yokes and were both surprised and elated at their success—some revolutions more successful than others. Joy turned to despair and despair to anger, however, as into the vacuum stepped highly organized Islamic movements. These Islamic parties were swept to power through democratic processes and then, ironically, used their mandate to impose Islamic law and with it, coercion. The possibility of freedom and its quick removal was, and is, more painful than the original oppression.

While the unfolding events may be ominous for human rights and basic freedoms, they are incredibly opportunistic for the gospel. Arab Muslims as a whole are disappointed and searching. For the first time, they are daring to think, seek, question, and search for ultimate answers—even outside of Islam. Never have we seen so much interest in the gospel, never have we seen so many Arab Muslims turn to Jesus. Now is the time to invest in the Arab world.

Live Dead as a specific missions strategy began in Sudan and was then broadened to include people groups across East Africa. The next Live Dead wave is the Arab world. Many organizations and missions have been active in the Arab world for decades, and Live Dead Arab World is intentional about Kingdom partnership with those already working in the Arab world, and those that will come.

The ultimate goal is to preach the gospel of the Kingdom among every people group on earth that Jesus might come back (Matthew 24:14). We believe the best way to do this is by working toward church-planting movements among every ethnolinguistic people. We want to link with others who share the same vision. We dedicate ourselves to God's team and His body as we pursue this common goal. Phase 1, already in motion, is a church-planting training team in Cairo. Phase 2 is church-planting teams in thirty-three gateway cities that have over one million people and are centers of commerce, culture, and influence; we have teams in four of these cities already. Phase 3 is a church-planting team among every people in the Arab world. Where others are already working, we will seek to join them; where we arrive first, we will open our hearts and homes to others.

The current instability of the Arab world is no deterrent. This is our new reality. The gospel must ever go forth under pressure. It is a joy and a privilege to lift up Jesus in an hour that is so precarious. The long-term safety of our teams is ever on our minds but not primary in our hearts. Our priority is to glorify God, proclaim the gospel boldly and widely, and allow God's character to be formed in us. Only after all of these are attended to do we consider our personal security and safety. As soon as our security becomes our initial priority, we will have missed what it means (and costs) to live dead, and we will not see the gospel preached in the Arab world, nor among every people, nor will the end come.

Live Dead in the Arab world is a joyful embracing of what will be—and its difficult means—for the joy set before us, for the glory of God among all peoples.

The Arab World

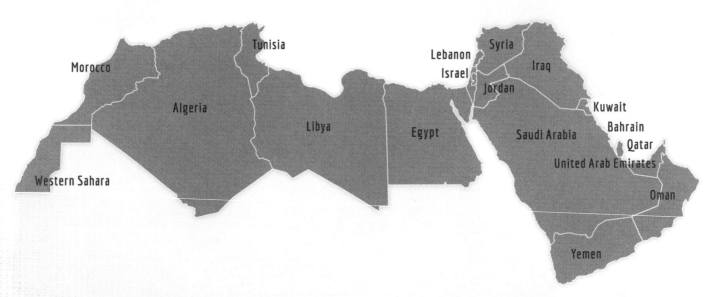

The gospel must ever go forth under pressure. It is a joy and a privilege to lift up Jesus in an hour that is so precarious.

— DICK BROGDEN & MARK RENFROE

WHAT SHOULD I EXPECT ON MY JOURNEY?

As you travel through this book, you will encounter sections asking you to perform journaling exercises. Don't feel inadequate or shy as you practice—there is not a right or wrong way to accomplish them. The exercises are designed to help you strengthen your own unique path and explore *your journey* in a fresh way as you travel through this book. As you read the art exercises, please remember you don't have to be an artist to fulfill them; you don't have to know how to draw or write. Use them to process what you are reading to expand your connection with the Muslim world that goes deeper through your senses. Take whatever it is God has gifted you with, and be an artist for *Him* so that you can grow closer in your walk and purpose. Through exploring the art exercises, you should find they will not only give you a deeper appreciation of the Muslim peoples, but that your passage through this book will be more enjoyable.

HOW SHOULD I APPROACH THE JOURNALING EXERCISES?

As you practice the journaling exercises, please remember:

1. **Keep it very simple or go all out.** Draw one line, or paint a portrait. Write one word, or compose a full poem. Do as little as you are prompted to do—or more.

2. **Don't over-think the exercises.** Feel open enough to write or illustrate the first thing that pops into your head.

3. **Feel free to make "mistakes."** Mistakes don't exist in this journey; they are simply experiments.

4. **Use your book as your canvas or get your own journal.** Be open to creativity and have an open mind. Track your moods, thoughts, and goals . . . just go for it!

Show off your work and create community: Share your work on our Live Dead Arab World Facebook page.

Be inspired, have fun, and play like the child God created you to be. In between chapters, feel motivated to have fun—dance, doodle, listen to music . . . who cares! Enjoy your journey into the Muslim world and use the artwork in the book to inspire you. Also, don't worry. Chances are, nobody is watching you except for the master Creator of all art, God Himself.

Judgment & Predestination

are two important beliefs within the

6 ARTICLES OF FAITH IN ISLAM

BELIEF IN
God

BELIEF IN
Al-Qadar
(Divine Predestination)

BELIEF IN
the Prophets

BELIEF IN THE
Day of Judgment

BELIEF IN THE
Divine Books

BELIEF IN
the Angels

Belief in a Judgment Day is widespread;

THE MAJORITY OF THE ARAB WORLD *holds the conviction that*

paradise awaits the faithful.

---

the *REALITY* of Islam

THE 5 PILLARS
of the faith

are devotional practices
considered nonnegotiable

FOR ALL MUSLIMS

1 DECLARATION OF FAITH IN GOD (ALLAH) AND THE PROPHET MUHAMMAD

97% of Muslims profess this to be true

FASTING DURING DAYTIME IN THE MONTH OF RAMADAN **2**

93% fast from sunup to sundown

3 OBSERVING ZAKAT (CHARITABLE GIVING)
77% faithfully give on a regular basis

PERFORMING SALAT (DAILY PRAYERS)
63% bow in prayer five times each day **4**

5 PILGRIMAGE TO MECCA (HAJJ)
9% journey to the sacred site

THE EXPRESSION "inshallah"

(IF GOD WILLS)

is a common figure of speech among Muslims
AND REFLECTS THE WIDESPREAD BELIEF THAT

{ *destiny is in the* HANDS OF GOD }

93% of Muslims in the Arab world *believe in predestination*

97% believe in heaven

90% believe in hell

ON AVERAGE

87% of Muslims in the Arab world believe religion is a vital part of their lives

Prayer needs no passport, visa, or work permit. There is no such thing as a "closed country" as far as prayer is concerned.

DAVID BRYANT

LIVE | DEAD

ARAB WORLD

I will intercede.

Write your prayer of intercession for Muslims here.

_____

_____

_____

_____

_____

_____

_____

_____

_____

_____

_____

KINGDOM PRAYERS: HOW TO PRAY FOR ARAB MUSLIM PEOPLES

BY DICK BROGDEN

Pray that the Holy Spirit would be poured out on all flesh.

Pray for God's Spirit to be poured out on Arab Muslims. Pray that old men, young women, poor grandmothers, and powerful businessmen will be overwhelmed by the Spirit. Pray for an outpouring of the Spirit on persecuted believers *and* on their persecutors. May new Pauls and new Peters arise from the Arab world—full of the Spirit of the fearless Savior.

Pray that the Lord of the Harvest would thrust forth workers into His harvest fields.

There are more than 350 people groups in the Arab world in need of workers. Pray God raises up multinational teams that embed themselves in each of these local communities, living the Kingdom, proclaiming the gospel, ministering to body, soul, and spirit, in sign, word, and deed.

Pray that the Word of God would rise.

Pray that God's Word would rise and cover the Arab world through the distribution of Scripture, radio and television broadcasts, printed literature, music, drama, storytelling, and all the creative arts. Pray that workers—foreign and national—would not speak their own words but would speak as oracles of God. Pray for the translation of the full Bible into every dialect spoken in the Arab world.

Pray that the Cross would be unveiled.

The god of this age has indeed blinded the eyes of our precious Arab Muslim friends. The Divine Christ, the Incarnate Word, the Atoning Savior, and the trustworthiness of the Scripture are all rejected by Arab Muslims. Pray that the veil would be lifted and God's salvation plan (in and through Jesus) would be made known. It will not be argument or force that prevails in the Arab mind and heart; it will only be God's unique revelation of Himself.

Pray that Christ would unite His body.

The American church is not going to reach the world. No single mission movement or country has the capacity to reach the unreached people that remain. No individual or church has the capacity to transform the Arab Muslim world. We are going to have to work together. We are going to have to submit to one another and lay down our cultural preferences, our nationalistic hubris, and our wills if the gospel will be preached in all the earth to all the nations. Our enemy knows this and works energetically to cause strife in missionary teams and suspicion among believers. Pray for unified teams. Pray for collaboration between mission agencies. Pray for trust among believers. Pray that Christ helps us over our foolish squabbles and joins us to His heart for His work.

Pray for the peace of Jerusalem and for men and women of peace.

Twenty years ago when I first ignorantly set out to assail the Muslim world, a Jewish believer in Christ gave me some precious wisdom. "Everyone who works with Arabs should pray for Jews, and everyone who works with Jews should pray for the Arabs," he advised as he gave me my first Arabic Bible. We take on the prejudices of the people we love. Pray that God's will is done in Israel and Jerusalem. Don't pretend to know what that is—just pray for God's peace.

In a similar vein, pray for persons of peace among the Arab Muslim peoples. Pray for persons of influence to be saved, those who can bring many others with them. Pray for those who own their own homes (and can host a house church); pray for those who own businesses (and can hire believers who lose their jobs); pray for the gatekeepers of communities who can open up whole tribes to the hearing of the gospel. Pray for men and women of peace who can become shepherds of the flock.

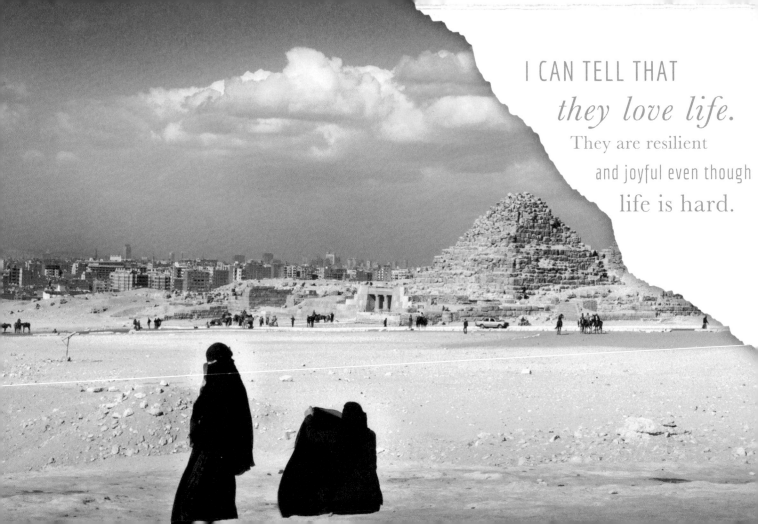

I CAN TELL THAT
they love life.
They are resilient
and joyful even though
life is hard.

FAITH JOURNEY

STOP ONE

A Walk Through Cairo

A WALK THROUGH CAIRO

During the day, Cairo's population grows to twenty-five million people. I see only a miniscule number of them. The medical clinic where I work is in a very poor suburb of the city, where most roads are unpaved, homes do not have running water, and only some have electricity.

I walk from the Metro train into the neighborhood. I pass street vendors selling onions, tomatoes, cucumbers, garlic, and fresh fruits, and because the clinic is in the area, I keep my eyes peeled for ladies that I know. Egyptians are very hospitable, and I enjoy the opportunity to visit their homes and talk with them. Often the conversations revolve around their families and the health of their children.

I reach the clinic and prepare for the day's work. We have an appointment with a family today about their seven-year-old son. Born with birth defects, he is paralyzed and unable to walk. The family is determined that he should walk, though there is nothing any doctor can do for him surgically. We pray for healing in Jesus' name often, and will continue to do so, even while we

CAIRO

start to teach him to use crutches and build his strength to use them, so he isn't crawling everywhere. The family has three younger children as well—the middle two are healthy, while the youngest has the same deformities as the eldest. I already expect my heart will break again when I see them today. I find myself simultaneously asking "Where is God in this?" while saying "All we have is God in this."

I look over at the flowers on the desk, and a smile takes over. The sister of the family coming today lives in the space above them. Her daughter had a heart defect. They brought the little girl to the clinic because of a cold, and we diagnosed her with a heart problem. (It's a crazy story.) We got her to a cardiologist and worked out the details for her successful surgery. Now everyone here says thank you, but this mother did something more—she brought me flowers. I know that she didn't have much money, but she gave me the flowers and said, "Thank you. You found this problem and helped us deal with it. You blessed our family." I've never had this happen before, and I will never forget it.

I probably shouldn't be too surprised. Even in this rough, poor neighborhood, the people are very happy. They love to laugh and have fun. Some ladies and I will go down to the Nile and have picnics of bread and cheese and water, and they will sit and tell jokes. I can tell that they love life. They are resilient and show great joy even though life is hard. I love witnessing the lives that can be helped with medicine, and I hurt with those that can't. I have shared many meals and a great deal of time with families, discussing how to deal with the difficulties, sharing Christ through all of it.

This neighborhood is only a small section of Cairo, but there are still a half-million people living here. There is never an end to the need. In the day-to-day work, it is an overwhelming task, and I cry, "God, how do we reach so many people?" The clinic sits within a circle of six mosques, and as I sit here with the windows open seeing patients all day (there is no air conditioning), I hear the call to prayer. It is right there in my face, and it is the loudest reminder of why I am here. I am here to proclaim Christ as loud as that call to prayer—I am to be as big a light and witness as that call to prayer, and it changes my cry to "God, you can reach so many people."

The very people I connect with each day are now standing up for freedom. Many have found themselves at Tahrir Square protesting for democracy. Recently, a vote did happen and the Muslim Brotherhood won a majority of the seats in the Egyptian assembly.

I'm often asked if I see the further Islamization of Egypt as a drawback to the people receiving the gospel message. It is harder to get into Egypt and share, but we are finding the people are more and more open. As the oppression of Islam becomes more severe, questions about God are more prevalent.

We believe Jesus came to save Egyptian Arabs. Go to your favorite news source and find out what is happening in Cairo today. Write a prayer for Egyptian Arabs who live in Cairo.

WHAT NOT TO PRAY FOR

Many Muslims come to faith as a result of Islamic fundamentalism. One pastor in Iran said, "The best missionary we ever had was the Ayatollah Khomeini." He meant, of course, that when radical Islam rises, it exposes what Islam really is and sets Muslims searching for something else, something of love, peace, and joy.

Over the last five decades, the great movements of Muslims to Christ have occurred where there was internecine Muslim violence. When a Muslim majority suppresses the rights of a Muslim minority (often violently), it always sours the Muslim minority on Islam and sets them on a path to seek answers elsewhere. This proved true in Indonesia (1960s), Bangladesh (1970s), Iraq and Iran (1980s), Algeria and Mauritania (1990s), and Darfur, Sudan (2000s).

We never wish protracted suffering on our brothers and sisters in the faith, but as an Eritrean pastor (still in prison) instructs us, "Don't pray that our persecution will end; pray that we will be faithful in persecution that many might come to know the Lord."

MEDITATION

The missionary writes, "Where is God in this?" while saying "All we have is God." What do you think this means? Have you ever asked yourself this? If so, write an example.

_____

_____

_____

_____

_____

_____

_____

_____

_____

JOURNALING

1) List four prayers God has answered for you throughout your lifetime.

---

2) Find an image or a simple word in a magazine that visually inspires you when you meditate on your answered prayers. Place or tape the word or image in your journal.

3) Take a moment to deeply thank and praise God for all He has done for you.

4) Optional: Take it to the next level, and draw, paint, or collage from the magazine images that compound what you have already written.

love is
THE ROOT
of missions;
sacrifice is
THE FRUIT
of missions.

— RODERICK DAVIS

FAITH JOURNEY

STOP TWO

The Value of Abiding

EXTRAVAGANT DAILY TIME WITH JESUS

BY DICK BROGDEN

You believe in a financial tithe. All your resources belong to God, and you return to Him a portion of what is already His. What about your time? Does it all belong to God? Should the principle of tithing apply to your time? How extravagant are you toward Jesus with your time? Do you lavish time on Jesus? Do you give Jesus the most energetic and focused times of your day? Or do you tend to give Jesus the crumbs of your schedule? Here is what I enjoy doing in my abiding time:

PRAYER

I have never been particularly good at sitting and praying. I need to pace, move, pray out loud—otherwise I get distracted; so I start my abiding time with a run—literally. I run two miles and then walk home. As I walk, I pray. I usually pray through the points of the well-known acronym ACTS.

- *Adoration* (15 minutes): I praise Jesus, love Him, exalt Him, worship Him for who He is, who the Bible says He is.
- *Confession* (15 minutes): I confess my sin and failures. I also confess who God is. I recite the Apostles' Creed. I often do this out loud—confessing to the powers in the heavens and the homies on the bike path the wonders of who Jesus is.

- ***Thanksgiving*** (15 minutes): I thank Jesus for His created world, for friends, family, favor, health, blessings. For the Holy Spirit, for the prevailing blood, for the Word, for all He has done and all He is.
- ***Supplication*** (15 minutes): I make my petitions known.

At the end of the ACTS prayer (and sometimes in the middle), I will also:

- pray in the Spirit (Ephesians 6:18), allowing the Holy Spirit to pray through me and build me up in the inner person.
- wait quietly on the Lord, trying not to say anything, but just to listen to what He wants to say to me.

BIBLE READING

For my time in the Word, I daily read six chapters: three chapters from the Old Testament, one from the Psalms, one from the Gospels, and one from the Epistles. I mark up my Bible like crazy, make notes in the margins, and try to summarize one key thought on top of each column. This usually takes about an hour.

SUPPLEMENTAL READING

I often read from a devotional or spiritual classic. François Fénelon, Oswald Chambers, Richard Foster, and C. S. Lewis are all favorites.

MEMORIZATION

I try to spend about five minutes a day memorizing Scripture.

PRAISE

I end my time by banging out some hymns and choruses on the piano. I sing and express my adoration to Jesus in somewhat off-key enthusiasm.

ABIDING LEADS TO FRUIT

BY DICK BROGDEN

"He who abides in Me and I in Him bears much fruit; for without Me you can do nothing." —JOHN 15:5 (NKJV)

Extravagant daily time with Jesus—this is the center of abiding. Not legalism, not dry discipline, not manufactured spirituality, but joyous soaking in the presence of Jesus, lavish spending of time with Him who is most precious, Him from whom all life flows. In a world that is overconnected yet lonely, frantically busy yet accomplishing little of eternal value, superinformed but egregiously ignorant on what really matters, abiding is a call to give Jesus the best of our time that He in turn leads us to the best of times.

GOD'S HEARTBEAT

The Bible is a missiological masterpiece. From beginning to end, God unveils His grand design to be glorified by every tribe, tongue, people, and nation. Missions is not a New Testament addition. Missions is God's heartbeat from Genesis to Revelation. The Gospel of John is no exception. John is full of non-Jews finding the Savior of the world. John repeats a "sending" motif: Jesus sent by the Father to save sinners, the disciples sent by Jesus to make disciples of all nations.

By the time we get to John 15, Jesus is at the end of His earthly ministry. The teaching of Jesus in John 15 takes place on the night He is arrested in Gethsemane. He is giving His disciples one last charge. He is pouring out His heart as to what is important. John uses the metaphor of the vine in harvest mode. Jesus is life (the vine), the Father sustains the vine and the vineyard, and the disciples are the branches. Branches are intended to bear fruit (other disciples), and are guaranteed to do so if they abide. Bearing fruit is in fact guaranteed (John 15:5) if the disciples abide. Let's look at the text to see what it teaches on the nature of abiding and fruit.

ABIDING

The Greek word for abiding (*meno*) is connected to the Latin *maneo*—meaning *house*. From it we derive the English *mansion*. Abiding means to remain in one place, at a given time, with someone, to dwell with someone. John uses *meno* to express a reciprocal indwelling: We are in Jesus and Jesus is in us. We linger in Him and He lingers in us. We live in Him and He lives in us. He is the source of life, He is the sap, and this interaction is both constant and with special times of union. It is both the journey and the destination.

Abiding is elongated, patient waiting in the presence of Jesus. Abiding is extravagant (concentrated) daily times with Jesus and all-day awareness. Abiding is constant communion in the midst of a crowded world and busy life and unique times of sweet, exclusive fellowship. Abiding implies extravagance. When John uses *meno*, there is always a sense of endurance, continuance, tarrying, and waiting with expectancy over time.

Men and women of God through the centuries have lived out this abiding truth. There are no heroes of the faith who did not live out this extravagant lavishing of their time on Jesus. When we examine their private lives, we see that they needed to abide for strength and wisdom. They were addicted to

DICK BROGDEN

My wife, Jennifer, and I have two sons, Luke and Zack—both born in the Sudan, a fact they are supremely proud of. We have been working among Muslims since 1992 (in Mauritania, Kenya, Sudan, and Egypt) and love it. We love Muslims. The more Arab Muslims we reunite with in heaven, the more spicy heaven will be. Abiding for us is not legalistic. Sure, we work at it—and some days we don't spend extravagant time with Jesus—but it is such a joy when we do. Discipline leads to desire, and desire to delight. Jesus is life, and there is no substitute for lingering in His presence, by His Spirit, in His Word.

My prayer for you is that God renews a desire in you to spend extravagant daily time with Him. If you do abide in Him and He in you, you will bear much fruit (John 15:5).

extravagant time in the presence of Jesus because it gave them life and joy and was the only thing that fulfilled them.

Abiding is both active and passive. Abiding is passive in the sense that Jesus pursues us and invites us to rest in His presence. Abiding is active in the reality that the spiritual disciplines position us to receive the life of Jesus—His heavenly sap. Discipline leads to desire, which matures into delight.

FRUIT

The Greek word for fruit is *karpos*. Scholars have assigned various meanings to *fruit* according to context, including Christlike character, confession of Christ's name in praise, contribution to those in need, conduct in general, and as those converted through one's witness. The New Testament has a variety of understandings for *fruit*.

John, however, has a distinct and sharply focused use of the word. Of the eleven uses of *karpos* in John (ten are in John 15 and one is in John 4), all can be understood to be in the context of harvest. *Karpos* literally means "that which is harvested—'harvest, crop, fruit, grain.' " The sense is an external yield that can be gathered. While not unique in the New Testament in this regard, John—especially in chapter 15 of his Gospel—seems to emphasize that the fruit of abiding is a harvest of people.

BUILDING BLOCKS

There is no standardized formula for abiding, but Scripture and the biographies of men and women through the ages point us to two nonnegotiables: the Word of God and prayer. Extended daily time in the Word and in the presence of Jesus through prayer are the basic building blocks of abiding.

Jesus spent close to 90 percent of His life in a village of twelve families, and even His three years of ministry were characterized by time alone with the Father. Moses spent forty years in Midian and had multiple trips to the mountain with God. Paul spent thirteen years in preparation, some of it in the Arabian Desert, and prayed constantly. Adam, Joseph, David, Elijah, Daniel, Mary, John, and others all gave God extravagant time. When we examine the lives of any heroes of the faith, we can see that they lingered daily with Jesus.

David Livingstone, the nineteenth-century pioneer medical missionary, once said, "Shall I tell you what sustained me amidst the trials and hardships and loneliness of my exiled life? . . . It was a promise, the promise of a gentleman of the most sacred honor. It was this promise: 'Lo, I am with you always, even unto the end of the world.' "

Discipline leads to desire, which matures into delight.

— DICK BROGDEN

John York, no stranger to pressure, dying too young from leukemia, expounds on Livingstone's thought and reminds us, "There is no 'Go' without 'Lo.' " First we are called to Jesus; He is with us always, and we with Him, then we go . . . to the uttermost parts and pressures of the earth. At Livingstone's death, his body was found bent in prayer, kneeling at his bed. His Bible was open to Matthew 28. In the margin was this small notation: "The word of a Gentleman."[1]

Eric Liddell of *Chariots of Fire* fame won a gold medal in the 1924 Olympics in the 400 meters—an event he had not trained for but ran in because his favored event, the 100-meter dash, was scheduled to be run on a Sunday. In 1925, Liddell went to China as a missionary. He was arrested by the Japanese occupiers and incarcerated in a concentration camp. A fellow prisoner watched him die and noted:

"What was his secret? He unreservedly committed his life to Jesus Christ as his Savior and Lord. That friendship meant everything to him. By the flickering light of a peanut-oil lamp early each morning, he studied the Bible and talked with God an hour every day. As a Christian, Eric Liddell's desire was to know God more deeply; and as a missionary, to make him known more fully."[2]

George Mueller is famed for a life of prayer, trusting God to provide food and finances for the hundreds of children sheltered in his orphanages. Mueller said, "I look upon it as a lost day when I have not had a good time over the Word of God."

When Mueller was in his eighties, he was asked by a group of seminary students, "Mr. Mueller . . . what is your secret?" He pushed his chair back and began to bend his old limbs to the floor as he knelt in prayer. "This," he said, "this is the secret."[3]

Mary Slessor was a fire-filled Scottish redhead accustomed to fighting thugs in Dundee with her fists. She went to Africa and fought slave traders and baby killers, giving her life to the Calabar people and fighting for the rights of African women. She lived for forty years in a mud hut, and thousands of Africans mourned her when she died in 1915. Her African name was "Mother of All Peoples." Mary cultivated a lifelong habit of chatting with her heavenly Father out loud and incessantly. It was Slessor who coined the phrase "God plus one are always a majority."[4]

MEDITATION

Reflect on how you spend extravagant time and abide in Jesus daily. What could you do to abide in the Lord more lavishly?

_____

_____

_____

_____

_____

_____

_____

_____

JOURNALING

1) Close your eyes and take a moment to think about what it means to abide in Jesus. How does this affect your personal relationship with Him? Open your eyes and write the first few words that came to mind.

_____

_____

_____

2) Write a short sentence or short poem using the words you chose. (No rhyming required.)

_____

_____

_____

_____

_____

3) Recite what you wrote as a declaration to the Lord.

THE EXCHANGED LIFE

BY DICK BROGDEN

"Every branch in Me that does not bear fruit He takes away." —JOHN 15:2A (NKJV)

If you are like me, you will have missed the fact that there are three types of branches in John 15. Most of us have noticed only two (both in verse 2): the branches "in Me that do not bear fruit that are taken away," and the branches "that bear fruit and are pruned." The third type of branch, however, is mentioned in verse 6. It is the branch that does not abide in Jesus and is cast out, withered, and burned. Let's begin by examining the first branch.

It seems strange that branches Jesus calls "in Me" should be "taken away." The Greek word translated by most translations as "take away" is αἴρω (*airo*). Interestingly, "take away" or "destroy" is not the primary meaning of *airo*. The primary meaning is to raise, elevate, or lift from the ground, to take upon oneself and carry, to bear what is raised and carry off.[5] Jesus is in fact saying, "Every disciple in Me who does not make disciples, the Father lifts up."

The study of viticulture gives us insight into what Jesus is trying to teach. In a vineyard, there are multiple reasons that the branches of the vine have to be lifted up. One is that some branches are weak and need to be lifted and tied to a trellis. Other branches have drooped into the mud and need to be lifted out of the damp soil. Others are not getting enough light and have to be brought up to where there is more light. Sometimes inclement weather has knocked branches down and the gardener lifts them and ties them to the trellis until they regain strength and healthy form.

In light of the New Testament use of *airo* to mean "lift," the circumstantial evidence of the verse (the branches in question are "in" Christ) suggests the branches that are not bearing fruit are being lifted up off the ground with the intention that they concentrate on gaining life from the vine so that they one day bear fruit.

This practice of "lifting" or "training" in viticulture suggests John's understanding that unfruitful disciples—those who are not reproducing disciples—need to be lifted out of their ministry context so they can be trained to draw life and strength for the future harvest. This was certainly the case for Hudson Taylor. A lifting was used to produce eventual fruit.

THE EXCHANGED LIFE

Taylor served as a missionary in China for six years, but returned to England because of illness. V. Raymond Edman (*The Disciplines of Life*) and F. J. Heugel (*Bone of His Bone*) pick up the story:[6]

". . . [H]e settled with his little family in the east end of London. Outside interests lessened; friends began to forget; and five long years were spent in the dreary street of a poor part of London, where the Taylors were 'shut up to prayer and patience.' From the record of those years it has been written, 'Yet, without those hidden years, with all their growth and testing, how could the vision and enthusiasm of youth been matured for the leadership that was to be?' There is the 'deep, prolonged exercise of a soul that is following hard after God . . . of a man called to walk by faith not by sight; the unutterable confidence of a heart cleaving to God and God alone, which pleases Him as nothing else can. Prayer was the only way by which the burdened heart could obtain any relief. And when the discipline was complete, there emerged the China Inland Mission, at first only a tiny root, but destined of God to fill the land of China with gospel fruit."

After Taylor returned to China, his colleague, a man by the name of Judd, remarked:

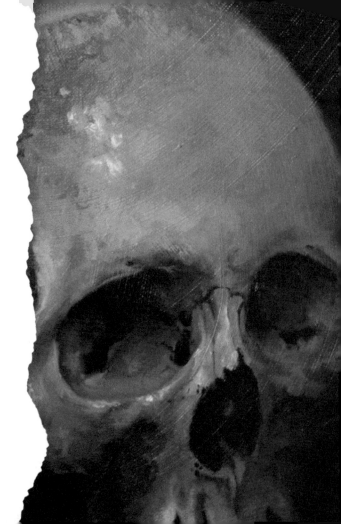

"He was a joyous man now, a bright, happy Christian. He had been a toiling, burdened one before, and latterly not much rest of soul. He was resting in Jesus now, and letting Him do the work—which makes all the difference.

"Whenever he spoke in meetings after that, a new power seemed to flow from him, and in the practical things of life a new peace pressed him. Trouble did not worry him as before.

"He cast everything on God in a new way, and gave more time to prayer. Instead of working late at night, he began to go to bed earlier, rising at 5 a.m. to give time to Bible study and prayer (often two hours) before the work of the day began.

"It was the exchanged life that had come to him—the life that is indeed 'No longer I.' "

Never pity missionaries; envy them. They are where the real action is—where life and death, sin and grace, heaven and hell converge. — ROBERT C. SHANNON

THE PRIVILEGE OF SUFFERING

BY DICK BROGDEN

"Every branch that bears fruit He prunes, that it may bear more fruit." —JOHN 15:2B (NKJV)

We have seen thus far that Jesus is the vine, disciples are the branches, and God the Father gardens in such a way (and with the intention) that every disciple bears disciples. The Father lovingly tends to disciples who do not produce disciples, orchestrating events so that they learn to draw life from Jesus (abide), as the fruit of making disciples is guaranteed if we will abide. The disciples who do bear disciples have an interesting reward: They get pruned.

The word for "prune" in Greek is καθαίρω (*kathairo*). Literally, *kathairo* means "I clean." Clearly Jesus' intention was a "cleaning" or "purifying" process for those who produce disciples, so they might produce more! John uses the same word for "prune" as he does for "washing" in the narrative of Jesus cleaning the disciples' feet. Cleaning is not to be understood as "ritual washing" in John's use, for it has the implication of purification through suffering, difficulty, and loss—which is why translators chose the word "prune" instead of "clean," as they wanted to indicate the purifying process of washing that occurs through discipline, hardship, and even suffering.

This reading is consistent with the parallel teaching of Paul: "In fact, everyone who wants to live a godly life in Christ Jesus will be persecuted" (2 Timothy 3:12) and "For it has been granted to you on behalf of Christ not only to believe in him, but also to suffer for him" (Philippians 1:29). The sense of John's text is branches prepared for greater fruit bearing by the cleansing of discipline, difficulty, and suffering.

According to Mark Edwards in his commentary on John,[7] by suffering, disciples of Jesus are cleansed and prepared for greater effectiveness just as He was. *Kathairo* in this context was also considered to imply suffering by Chrysostom (who considered it the tribulation that follows the death of Christ), Elsley (who interpreted it as the removal of false opinions), and Augustine (who cited 1 John 1:8 to prove that we all need cleansing).

John's use of "pruning" implies a cleansing through difficulty, which results in the disciple bearing more disciples than he or she had before. One divine purpose in the suffering of God's people is empowerment—suffering empowers us to better make disciples.

John Piper sums up this idea in *A Holy Ambition:* "Suffering is not only the consequence of completing the Commission, but it is God's appointed means by which he will show the superior worth of his Son to all the peoples. Just as it was 'fitting that he . . . should make the founder of [our] salvation perfect through suffering' (Hebrews 2:10), so it is fitting that God save a people from all the peoples from eternal suffering through the redemptive suffering of Jesus displayed in the temporal suffering of his missionaries. . . . What is lacking in Jesus' sufferings is not their redemptive value but their personal presentation to the peoples he died to save."[8]

One divine purpose
in the suffering of
God's people
is empowerment—
suffering
empowers us
to better
make disciples.

— DICK BROGDEN

THE PROOF OF DISCIPLESHIP

BY DICK BROGDEN

"If anyone does not abide in Me, he is cast out as a branch and is withered; and they gather them and throw them into the fire, and they are burned." —JOHN 15:6 (NKJV)

At this juncture, John introduces a third branch. The first branch (15:2a) is in Christ but not producing disciples. That branch will be nurtured and taught to abide so that divine life will flow and disciples will be made. The second branch (15:2b) is the disciple of Christ who does make disciples. This disciple is disciplined, allowed to pass through difficulty and suffering, that he or she might be even more effective in making disciples. The third branch (15:6) is the disciple who does not lavish on Jesus extravagant daily time.

The consequences for the third branch are sure and shockingly swift. The immediate effect of "not abiding" is the absence of divine life, which quickly leads to being thrown outside, apart from the source of life. The disciple who does not abide is allowed to fall (the Greek word translated "cast out" can also be translated "fall") from the vine to the ground and to be cast into the fire (also translated as "place of punishment or shame"). Withered branches are stiff or rigid. Rigid, stiff branches are unable to draw life from the vine and thus dry up. The vinedresser lets them fall out, and eventually they dry up and are ignited, burned until they are consumed. In what seems to be a negative cyclical combination, inflexibility and rigidity hinder abiding, and lack of abiding results in inflexiblity and rigidity.

Branches are not forced to abide. We are not forced to spend extravagant daily time with Jesus, but if we don't we *will* become so dry that we separate from the vine. We will be burned (disposed of) as we are not accomplishing our intended purpose (bearing disciples) and so are good for nothing.

In Jesus' missiological thinking, disciples are sent to harvest disciples. The power to harvest disciples comes from giving extravagant time to Jesus on a daily basis in order to draw life from Him. Disciples who do not lavish extravagant daily time on Jesus will not harvest disciples, and the Father then lifts them out of ministry so they can learn to abide in Him (for the eventual purpose of harvesting disciples)—this is the first branch.

Disciples who do not respond to this grace period, this invitation to focus on drawing life from Jesus, eventually become hard, stiff, and resistant to God's overtures, so He lets them fall to the ground where they wither and disconnect themselves from the vine. There is nothing left for them but to be gathered and burned.

Disciples who do lavish extravagant daily time on Jesus will harvest disciples, and their reward is the joy of participating in the sufferings of Christ with the

purpose of being used to bring even more disciples into the Kingdom. In God's great master plan, the harvest cycle continues (John 15:16) as those disciples brought to faith by disciples in turn learn to abide, which has the promise of them also participating in harvest.

"If you abide in Me, and My words abide in you, you will ask what you desire, and it shall be done for you. By this My Father is glorified, that you bear much fruit; so you will be My disciples" (John 15:7-8 NKJV).

There are two essential spiritual disciplines to abiding, both mentioned in the verses above. The first is the Word of God. Our abiding in Jesus and God's words abiding in us are inseparably linked. When the Word of God abides (dwells, lives, remains, continues) in us, then our prayers are answered. Abiding may indeed vary from person to person, but for all it must center on the life of Jesus as expressed through His Word and our prayer. This prayer, according to Jesus, is inescapably linked to mission. "You did not choose Me, but I chose you and appointed you that you should go and bear fruit, and that your fruit should remain, that whatever you ask the Father in My name, He may give you" (15:16).

"Notice the amazing logic of this verse," John Piper writes in *A Holy Ambition*. "He gave them a mission 'in order that' the Father would have prayers to answer. This means that prayer is for mission. It is designed to advance the kingdom."[9]

When we abide with Jesus, when we lavish extravagant daily time on Him, we get a pretty good idea of what He wants. He wants us to bear disciples. After all, that is what He told us to do in the Great Commission: Make disciples of everyone, everywhere! God is glorified when we bear many disciples. It is in glorifying God (by lavishing extravagant time on Jesus, having His Word abide in us, asking Him for the things on His heart, and bearing many disciples) that we become disciples.

The Greek text in John 15:8 indicates a process: As we obey God and make disciples, we become disciples. Making disciples is then, in essence, proof that we are disciples. Our own discipleship is an ongoing formation, and as we glorify the Father—by abiding in Jesus, allowing His Word to abide in us, praying for the things on His heart, and bearing many new disciples—we both are and increasingly become His disciples.

MEDITATIONS

Jesus is the vine, and we are His branches. When we are not producing fruit (making disciples), God loves us so much that He coordinates trials in our lives that are often painful. But if we allow God to work, in the end these hardships mature us spiritually.

List at least one time over the past year when God has pruned your branches. What was the result?

_____

_____

_____

_____

_____

_____

_____

_____

JOURNALING

1) Find a magazine. Tear out an image that makes you think of God pruning His branches. Place or tape the image in your journal.

2) Write one of your favorite Scriptures around the picture, and thank God for shaping you to be a better disciple for Him.

3) Pray that Arab Muslim peoples would follow Jesus and become fruitful branches for Him.

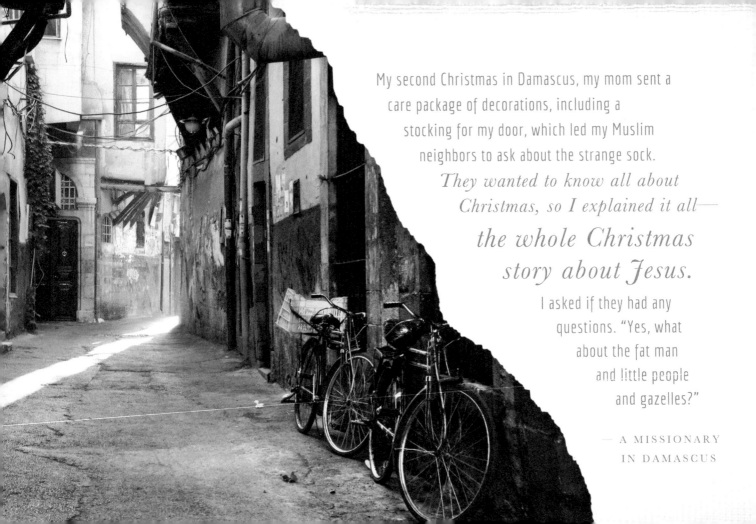

My second Christmas in Damascus, my mom sent a care package of decorations, including a stocking for my door, which led my Muslim neighbors to ask about the strange sock. *They wanted to know all about Christmas, so I explained it all—* **the whole Christmas story about Jesus.** I asked if they had any questions. "Yes, what about the fat man and little people and gazelles?"

— A MISSIONARY
IN DAMASCUS

STOP THREE

A Walk Through Damascus

A WALK THROUGH DAMASCUS

I used to live in Damascus. During a recent visit with my neighbor, I discovered that her sister and children had just arrived from there. The situation in Syria is so dangerous now that the woman's husband sent them to this nearby country. My heart sank into my stomach. Each day as the unrest continues in Syria and the fighting rages in Damascus, I get more concerned for my dear friends, the Muslim family that lived across the hall.

I love that family. They adopted me into theirs while I lived there. Where most Syrians seemed afraid of me at first, this family opened their arms to me from the beginning. Their door was always open to me, and I visited them four or five times a week getting help with my Arabic. This family was my family. If I had to go to the airport, they took me. I played with their two kids. The wife taught me how to make Arab food. We chatted for hours and hours; they were fascinated by America, and I wanted to know more about Arab culture. I even served as the chaperone for the man's teenage nieces. And now I wonder where they all are.

I think about my favorite stories of them, to keep my mind on pleasant things. There was the day they took me to the market. I got ready, and as I waited for a knock on my door, I started playing my keyboard. I didn't realize they were in the hallway and could hear me. I stopped playing, wondering what was keeping them. After a couple of minutes, they knocked. "You stopped playing," they said. "We never heard music like that before." They had been outside, just listening to me. The best part of the story is that for months I had struggled to construct sentences and carry on conversation in Arabic. But as we walked through the market, I told them about the music I was playing, why I was playing it, and for whom I was playing. That night I shared the entire gospel with them. It was the first time I ever shared the gospel in Syria *and* the first time ever in Arabic. It was divine intervention, because it was so far beyond my Arabic abilities to share all of that. I got home and thought, "What in the world was I even saying?"

I remember my Christmases there. My second Christmas in Damascus, my mom sent a care package of decorations, including a stocking for my door, which led them to ask about the strange sock. They wanted to know all about Christmas, so I explained it all—the whole Christmas story about Jesus. I asked if they had any questions. "Yes, what about the fat man and little people and gazelles?" I smile now, but my response then was, "Really? That's your question?"

Life in Damascus was often like that: amusing, surprising, and interesting. I found one of the best places for amusement and interest was in the Old City at the Souk El-Hamidiyeh, a huge market and one of the oldest in the world. It is a labyrinth of interesting things that goes for miles in every direction. I wandered through that market for hours shopping and meeting different people. I wonder what it looks like now, and how many people are still wandering its alleyways. I remember the man in a fez hat near the entrance to the market. He carried a giant pot of coffee on his back and poured the coffee from the pot into little cups for people to drink. He clinked the cups together to get people's attention. I was never a customer; the idea of communal cups kept me away.

I could have two different experiences at the market depending on how I dressed. I only spoke in Arabic, so all that mattered was whether my hair showed or not. As soon as they looked at me, they knew I was not Arab. If I had my hair completely covered, they assumed I was half-Arab or very fair because they could not see my hair. In that case they would treat me like any other Arab. I got better prices, and the men never looked at me, but we did bargain. When my head was uncovered, they dealt with me very differently. I could be friendlier in a way, but I was also harassed more. I normally only went with my head uncovered if I wanted to practice my Arabic, and I had some fun conversations that way. There were a few shop owners that let me sit and talk with them. Once a week, I stopped to visit and have tea with one particular shop owner. All the items in this man's shop were handmade in Syria, and he would tell me where each thing came from and show me old money from different places. He was so kind and so intriguing.

His shop was right in front of the Umayyad Mosque, which is one of the holiest mosques in Islam and where Muslims believe Jesus will return. Covered in my long polyester coat and hijab, I visited the mosque often. This mosque has several distinct areas in it. I talked to people visiting the tomb of Saladin, the champion of Muslims during the Crusades. The head of Hussein, the grandson of Muhammad, is there, and I sat for hours with women who were distraught and needing God to intervene. In the main room is a shrine with the head of John the Baptist. I went to the back of the room where the women were and discussed the Qur'an and the Gospels and John the Baptist with them, and inevitably, no matter how I timed it, the call to prayer always went off. The entire room stopped to pray, heads to the floor, and I watched them go through their prayers.

This was my life in Damascus, one of the oldest continually inhabited cities in the world. Imagine—a city with people living in it for 5,000 years or more. When I lived there, the city seemed to straddle the fourteenth and twenty-first centuries. I bought my vegetables from a cart pulled by a donkey, ridden by a man talking on his cell phone. Now I read that there were attacks near the Umayyad Mosque and see images in the news of empty streets, closed shops, and bombed buildings in different Damascus neighborhoods.

I pray for my family. I might have no way to reach them, but I trust God knows how.

God isn't looking for **PEOPLE OF** *great faith,* but for individuals **READY TO** *follow Him.*

— HUDSON TAYLOR

FAITH JOURNEY

STOP FOUR

The Value of Community

EXTRAVAGANT DAILY TIME WITH JESUS

BY EVA BRIDGES

My husband will tell you that he never speaks to me in the morning before I've had my coffee and my Jesus time. I'm simply not a nice person before Jesus washes me of myself and pours His Spirit over me. So I get up early every morning, make a cup of French press coffee, and then go over my Scripture memorization cards. I try to memorize a new verse each week in English and Arabic.

I then read a portion of Scripture. Because I am a creative person, I've learned that one-year Bible plans and devotionals simply don't work for me. I need variety and spontaneity to keep my relationship with Jesus fresh. Sometimes I study a single person in the Bible for several weeks. Sometimes I focus on one verse, meditate on it, and then write in my journal. Sometimes I read an entire book of the Bible at one time. I usually end this time by reading authors such as A. W. Tozer, C. S. Lewis, or John Eldredge.

After reading from the Word, I move to my prayer time. Because my brain wanders, I try to focus my prayer time. I've developed a weekly schedule so that I'm sure I pray for all those in my life each week. However, I do allow my mind the freedom to express my prayers in a variety of ways. Sometimes when I pray, I am inspired to write poetry. Other times, I lie on my face in my prayer room as I intercede for those around me. Sometimes I sit and stare at the maps on the wall showing countries we've lived in and listen to God's heart for the people in those areas. Although I am disciplined in having this time with Jesus, my abiding time is fluid. I generally don't worry about the time and rarely look at a clock. I simply continue in this time of prayer until I feel released in my spirit to begin my day.

One thing I have discovered is that I can't survive throughout the day on just one block of time with Jesus. So at some other point in my day, I spend time basking in His presence. Some days are busy, so this time may be only a few minutes. Other days are more flexible and free and I have the luxury of spending another thirty minutes with Jesus. Most of the time, this means sitting at my keyboard and playing whatever my fingers decide to play and my voice decides to sing. Sometimes, though, I write or sketch or just look at my flowers on the balcony. At other times, I go on prayer walks by myself or with a likeminded friend. This time is simply a time to love Jesus and allow His love to pour over me.

For me, abiding isn't only about the time in the morning when I pray and read. Abiding is a lifestyle. Abiding is praying for the lady who cuts me off on a busy street. Abiding is praying for the guy who is saying inappropriate things to me. Abiding is Jesus living through me. At times, I fail miserably and allow my flesh to overtake the situation. But at other times, I know the Spirit of God is at work in me so that He can work through me.

MEDITATIONS

Do you ever find yourself so wrapped up in your own life and work that your spiritual eyes are closed to those around you who may need encouragement or support? Take time to ask God to open your spiritual eyes.

JOURNALING

1) Look at your recent photos, and make a list of the last ten people with whom you were in community.

_____

_____

2) Community takes time. Out of the ten people you listed, which three do you feel God is asking you to invest time in?

_____

_____

3) Print out the three photos, and post them in your journal. Beside the photo, write specifically how you are going to respond to God's call to be in community with them.

59

COMMUNITY AND A PERSON OF PEACE

BY EVA BRIDGES

"When you enter a house, first say, 'Peace to this house.'" —LUKE 10:5

I could take you to the restaurant in Damascus where I had an epiphany experience regarding community in the Middle East. I was having coffee with my friend Ala', who was telling me about her recent arranged engagement. I was outraged inside that this brilliant, beautiful, talented woman wasn't allowed to choose her own husband, so I asked her how she felt about having her family arrange her marriage. She tilted her head and looked at me quizzically as she told me that she trusted her family to raise her, decide what schools to attend, and what to study. It only made sense that she would trust her family to decide this most important decision of her life. Then she went on to say the elders in her family decided these things for the good of the entire family.

At its core, true community comes through love. Ala' accepted her family's decisions because they were founded in her family's love for her and her love for them. Without a love for others, you will never truly live in community with others. Without a love for those around you, you will never enjoy the benefits, privileges, and joy that come with community. But community that comes through a love from the Father brings untold riches to your heart and life.

OUR BEST EXAMPLE

Although there are many resources available about developing community, the best and most notable resource on the subject is Jesus Himself. He is the greatest developer of community the world has ever known. Let's look at what Jesus asked of His followers as it relates to entering and joining a community.

Most of the time when we think of Jesus' community, we picture Him with His twelve disciples. This passage in Luke 10, however, speaks of seventy-two of Jesus' followers. These people had obviously been with Him for some time because He trusted them enough to send them ahead of Him to the surrounding areas. They had walked with Him as He preached throughout Judea and Galilee. These followers had heard His teachings and could speak on His behalf in new towns and villages. Jesus' decision to send the seventy-two was by no means random. On the contrary, He assigned each pair a specific town to visit.

The church has worked for centuries to create methods to reach the lost. We've gone door to door sharing the gospel. We've built tents and preached the Word. Although these are valid means of sharing the truth, what Jesus asked His followers to do was quite different. He actually forbade them from going house to house. Instead, He instructed them to locate homes and men of peace. This is no easy task—which is why He stresses the importance of prayer beforehand.

Prayer is every bit as active as sharing the gospel with someone. Prayer changes things. With much prayer come amazing supernatural feats that go beyond your wildest imaginations. We all understand the importance of a personal prayer life. However, praying with others connects minds and hearts in ways a conversation can't. The amazing thing is that a person doesn't have to be a follower of Christ to pray. You can pray with your person of peace over various concerns in his or her life, and then leave it up to God and see what He will do.

Jesus asked His followers to locate men and homes of peace because building community with a person of peace goes farther than just that individual. Jesus was starting a new movement. To do so, He needed as many people to hear the truth as possible. So, He developed a system whereby His followers told one family and then that family told people in their community, and on and on it went.

EVA BRIDGES

For my husband and me, our love story really began with separate lives of ministry in the Middle East. We both served as single workers for several years, Adam in Palestine and I in Lebanon and Syria. Then, by God's divine grace and mercy, He brought our hearts, lives, ministries, and love for Muslim Arabs together in Amman, Jordan. We are privileged to be vessels God uses to share His story with them.

Living in community is difficult for those from Western cultures. It takes intentional thought and action. For us, it means dying to ourselves daily as we reach beyond our introverted natures to intertwine our lives with those around us. Some days it is easier than others to close our computers, answer the door, and allow a neighbor in to spend an afternoon chatting over tea. Our prayer for you is that as you abide in Christ, God will open your eyes to see beyond your own doors to those all around you who need the loving hand of friendship.

Your person of peace has a network of others who need to hear the truth as well. In effect, the more time you spend with your person of peace, the more opportunities you have to share the truth with him. Then, your person of peace can share the truth with those in his circle. In essence, you'll be affecting the lives of countless people as you invest in your person of peace.

MY PERSON OF PEACE

Fatima is my person of peace. Honestly, she's the last person I would have chosen. A preschool teacher, she doesn't have an influential job. She's not a leader in the community or even the leader of our building. She's not even his wife. Instead, she's his daughter. But she is the one whom God has placed in front of me. So we meet together to talk as she's discovering that she's a sinner in need of a Savior. We've developed a trust, and now she comes to me to share her concerns and needs. She's looking for a listening ear and the knowledge that someone is praying for her.

What I find most interesting about our relationship is that although she has not given her heart to Jesus yet, she is constantly bringing other people to my home. She has a network of young women who are desperate for relationships, and Fatima sees me as the answer to that problem. I pray that Fatima discovers the truth, but until that time I am thankful for her connections and willingness to bring me into her world. In a place where everything is done in community, I trust that one day she and many of her friends will find the truth together.

MEDITATIONS

Do you currently have a person of peace in your life? How can you be more open as God leads you to a person of peace?

_____

_____

_____

_____

What are you doing to engage in community? Don't be afraid to share with others out of a place of vulnerability and honesty.

_____

_____

_____

_____

JOURNALING

1) List five of the most important factors about engaging in community.

_____

_____

_____

_____

_____

2) Pray that Christ would unite His body and allow for these factors to come alive in your life and in the Arab Muslim world.

_____

_____

_____

_____

COMMUNITY AND MENTORING

BY EVA BRIDGES

When they had crossed, Elijah said to Elisha, "Tell me, what can I do for you before I am taken from you?" "Let me inherit a double portion of your spirit," Elisha replied. —2 KINGS 2:9

Mentoring is more than just instilling a few skills and ideas into a person's life. Mentoring is about living life with that person. Mentoring is about being vulnerable and allowing that person to see you for who you really are, faults and all. When done well, mentoring should change the person being mentored and the mentor himself.

Today's journey in our discovery of community takes us to ancient Israel. The northern kingdom has been riddled with assassinations and war as men vie for power. Finally, an army officer named Omri declares himself king and takes over the throne. He arranges for his son, Ahab, to marry a Phoenician princess named Jezebel to ensure trade routes with this important area. Through this alliance, Israel gains much wealth, and in this time of prosperity Ahab succeeds his father to the throne.

But along with material wealth, Israel's alliance with Phoenicia also brings idol worship. Jezebel, queen of Israel, demands the people worship Baal. Enter Elijah.

Nothing is said in Scripture about Elijah's background except that he's a Tishbite and a settler in Gilead. In our first encounter with him, he is confronting Ahab for his idol worship (1 Kings 17). After Elijah declares a drought, which lasts three-and-a-half

Mentoring is about being vulnerable and allowing that person to see you for who you really are, faults and all. When done well, mentoring should change the person being mentored and the mentor himself.

— EVA BRIDGES

years, it ends in a beautiful picture of God's power over Baal at Mount Carmel (1 Kings 18). Elijah flees for his life to Horeb, where the Lord passes by him in a whisper (1 Kings 19). God then speaks to him about his future and who will succeed him.

Elijah throws his mantle over Elisha as a symbol of God's call. By accepting this symbol, Elisha is saying he accepts the arrangement. He is wholly committed. He sells everything he has, leaves his family, and starts walking with Elijah.

As you continue to pray for your person of peace, also pray for God to put an Elisha in your life. Your person of peace is a person who needs the truth; your Elisha is a person who walks with you in life to discover what God has for him or her. Your person of peace takes the truth to others; your Elisha goes with you on your journey.

Jesus' followers were His Elishas, who were then empowered to find people of peace. In the same manner, your Elisha should accompany you as you share with your person of peace. Both people of peace and Elishas are necessary as we work together to bring as many people into eternity with us as we can. This is only done as we commit to truly live together in community.

For ten years, Elisha walks with Elijah. From 1 Kings 20 through 2 Kings 2, Elisha witnesses miracles performed by God through Elijah. Scripture doesn't tell us much about their relationship, but we can assume that they spent many hours together walking the roads of the country. Elisha witnessed the supernatural and miraculous events in Elijah's life as well as the mundane.

MY ELISHA

My friend Zira was my Elisha. We met through a series of divine coincidences through another foreign friend. Zira was alone, living in a huge city, and struggling just to survive every day. When we met, she was living meal to meal, praying for God's divine provision. She was an excellent cook, so I asked her to teach me to make Arab food and hired her to cook when I had parties and hosted events. In the Middle East, work can never really be started until you've chatted about life over a cup of tea, so we started getting to know each other. One day, she saw my Arabic Bible sitting on my coffee table and asked me what it was. As it dawned on her what this green book was, tears began

streaming down her face. Finally, she asked if it was the words of Jesus. When I told her it was, she began to weep and to tell me her story.

Zira is from a prominent Muslim family. They're extremely devout and adhere to all the laws of Islam. Zira covered her hair, fasted during the month of Ramadan, gave alms to the poor, and prayed five times every day. But her heart was restless, and she began to wonder if Islam was really the way to God. She began doing something very small, but very bold: At the end of each of her prayers every day, she asked God to show her the truth. Because our God is faithful, one afternoon as she got up from her prayers, Jesus was standing in front of her. That day, she became a follower of Christ. She had never met a Christian or seen a Bible. All she knew was that Jesus was the Truth she had been looking for.

When her family discovered that she had left Islam, they were extremely upset. She had shamed them, and they told her that if she didn't turn back to Islam they would kill her. When I met her, she was in hiding from her family.

For weeks, we met together as she discovered who Jesus really is and what it means to follow Him. We simply lived life together. If I was going to meet with a neighbor, I brought her with me. If I was going on a prayer walk, she joined. We read the Scriptures together and talked about the early church and the struggles it endured.

Then one day, her family found where she had been hiding. They took her back to her village and turned me in as a missionary. Just before I was forced to leave the country, she called to let me know she was all right. Her family was beating her every day, trying to convince her to renounce her faith in Jesus and return to Islam. But she remembered our conversations about the persecution of the early church and was standing firm. She asked me not to pray against the persecution, but to pray that her family would see Jesus in her through it. Then she quoted 2 Corinthians 4:17: "For our light and momentary troubles are achieving for us an eternal glory that far outweighs them all."

Elijah's greatest accomplishment wasn't his ability to call down fire from heaven at Mount Carmel. It wasn't raising the widow's son from the dead. Instead, I would venture to say his greatest accomplishment was Elisha. For long after Elijah was taken to heaven, Elisha was continuing to do the work of the Lord. He was steadfast in his faith. He was strong, bold, and courageous. He affected eternity.

MEDITATIONS

Who is your Elijah? Thank this person this week for investing in you.

_____

_____

Who is your Elisha? How are you being intentional this week in blessing this person?

_____

_____

_____

_____

_____

_____

_____

JOURNALING

1) Draw a tree. Remember, simple works. One line with "branches" is all you need!

2) On two of the branches of the tree, write the names of your Elijah and your Elisha.

3) In a different color, draw three leaves next to each of the names you have written.

4) In the leaves by your Elijah, write things you are thankful for in this person.

5) In the leaves by your Elisha, write ways you can bless him or her this week.

6) Pray for God to bless your relationships with your Elijah and your Elisha.

COMMUNITY AND THE CHURCH

BY EVA BRIDGES

"By this everyone will know that you are my disciples, if you love one another." —JOHN 13:35

A few years ago, I had the privilege of visiting Cappadocia, Turkey. Not a popular tourist destination, to be sure, but it was incredible. During the Roman Empire, Christians fled to Cappadocia to escape persecution. They developed entire underground cities that included churches, ventilation chimneys, water wells, and toilets. Truly, it is mindboggling to see what our forefathers were able to create out of mud.

These underground cities were community at its core. It is believed that tens of thousands of our early forefathers and their families dwelled in these amazing underground structures as they tried to stay alive amid untold persecution. They lived life completely together, knowing that if someone betrayed them, all would be lost. However, life together in community began for them before they moved underground. It was part of the culture of the early church.

It's important to note that the early church grew by leaps and bounds. In Acts 1:15, there were 120 people in the Upper Room on the Day of Pentecost. By Acts 2:41, they had grown to an unbelievable 3,000. There was simply no way for the apostles to effectively meet the needs of 3,000 people at one time. Thus, in Acts 2:46, we see the new believers meeting together to express their corporate unity and breaking up into smaller, more manageable groups for the breaking of bread together.

We see in Acts a picture of believers meeting in homes as they discover together what it means to be followers of Christ. We see them conducting spiritual aspects of life together through prayer, and then we see them living life together through the breaking of bread. They were a close-knit group of people. They were in each other's lives every day. If they had had phones, they would've called and texted each other. If they had had Facebook, they would've written encouraging words and Scripture on each other's walls. They went to the market together, they ate together, they prayed together, they fasted together. Do you see a commonality? Everything they did was together. Life is meant to be lived with others.

However, what's amazing is that they weren't exclusive. "And the Lord added to their number daily those who were being saved" (Acts 2:47). It's easy to stick with your group. These are people you know. These are people who know you. You're comfortable there. However, God's love is not exclusive. His grace is for all. What I see in the early church is a contagious faith and an unwavering love that was a testimony of Jesus to those who had not yet heard the truth. "By this shall all men know that you are my disciples, if you have love for one another."

Community is not a feeling of belonging. Community is a deep unity. Have you ever heard a beautiful piece performed by a professional orchestra? Each instrument knows its part. The flutes tease our ears with a quick melody. The timpani's deep tones radiate through our core. The trumpets blast and the violins sing. Each instrument alone would sound strange and empty. Together, however, they create something that speaks more than words. This is life in community.

Community is each person knowing his or her place. It is each individual watching for the cue of the conductor to begin his part. And it is watching the smile on Jesus' face as we all work together to create seemingly impossible things we can only imagine.

Community is sharing together. We should be drawn together as believers because of God's grace through Christ (Philippians 1:7 and Romans 6:3-4). We have a common inheritance as sons and daughters of the Most High that should lead to worship and prayer together.

Community is sharing outwardly together in common service. Grace is not only for believers. God's love is not exclusive. The truth should be given to others. It is through outreach that the community of believers helps to reconcile to God those far from Him.

OUR IMMEDIATE COMMUNITY

When we first moved into our apartment, many of our neighbors were concerned about having Americans in the building. They've seen American television and movies and assumed our lives would be similar. They worried about whom we might bring into the building and what that would mean for their own families. Thus, they decided that they would be nice to us, but not really get to know us.

We, however, were committed to living in community with our neighbors. We desired to live openly with them. We made intentional decisions about where we would live, how we would furnish our home, and how we would dress. Each decision, although seemingly insignificant, was so that those in our community would feel comfortable in our home and see us as moral and good people.

From the very beginning, we visited each neighbor with a plate of American goodies. I learned a long time ago that chocolate-chip cookies will soften anyone's heart. Several times a week, I set aside time for visiting with the ladies in my building. We talk about life, they teach me Arab dishes, and I teach them American desserts. They help me with my Arabic, and I help them with their English.

Now I consider many of them as part of our family. They know they can drop in anytime, and we can do the same. Our lives are intertwined as we live together in community. Even as I type this, I am interrupted by a neighbor who simply wants to talk over a cup of tea. These neighbors share their needs, and we commit to pray for them. And because we live so closely together, they often comment on our commitment to God and our moral lifestyle, which gives us the perfect opportunity to share about our love for Jesus. Life in community creates space for the Holy Spirit to work in the hearts of those around us.

MEDITATIONS

Are you creating space in your life for community? Evaluate your life and schedule this week. How can you create more community in your everyday life?

_____

_____

_____

_____

_____

_____

_____

_____

JOURNALING

1) Text or email someone you have been too busy to share fellowship with and ask him or her to lunch or coffee.

2) Write his or her name in your journal and circle it as you pray that God would help you to reach out to others more.

We must be ready to allow ourselves to be interrupted by God. We must not . . . assume that our schedule is our own to manage, but allow it to be arranged by God.

— DIETRICH BONHOEFFER

STOP FIVE

The Role of the Holy Spirit as Guide

THE ROLE OF THE HOLY SPIRIT AS GUIDE

BY MARK RENFROE

Austin is praying about joining a Live Dead Arab World church-planting team, but he is worried that this is simply an emotional response.

Dear Austin,

Live Dead is all about hearing the voice of the Holy Spirit and then radically following Him in obedience. I don't really see this as something for special Christians. The New Testament seems to indicate that this is meant to be normative for followers of Jesus. However, discerning the will of God involves several different elements. Here is what I recommend as you seek God concerning when and if you should join one of our church-planting teams in the Arab world.

First, remember that the Holy Spirit is a person, not a thing. You get to know the voice of God the same way you get to know anyone—by spending time with Him. There is simply no substitute for giving the best of your day to abiding in the presence of Jesus. It is there that He speaks through His Spirit.

Second, our heavenly Father is good. Maybe that sounds simplistic, but I have talked to so many believers through the years who seem to suffer from a "Jonah complex"—constantly fearing that God is going to call them to do something that they don't want to do. Luke 11:11-14 directly links the goodness of the Father to the work of the Holy Spirit. The Holy Spirit only guides us to those places where our loving and good heavenly Father is waiting for us.

Next, the Holy Spirit leads through the counsel of other believers. Acts 15:28 says, "It seemed good to the Holy Spirit *and* to us" (emphasis mine). The leaders of the early church understood that there was value and safety in the collective wisdom of the body of Christ. Talk to the godly men and women in your life. Radical obedience creates a greater interdependence on fellow believers—not less.

Finally, we must remember that there is no place for a believer saying no to the voice of the Holy Spirit. A. W. Tozer has been quoted as saying, "Christians don't tell lies—they go to church and sing them." How often do we call Jesus "Lord" and yet refuse to obey His Word. Personally, I want to be that man who listens carefully to the voice of the Shepherd and then runs in obedience.

May God give you ears that are sensitive to the voice of the Holy Spirit and feet that are quick to obey.

Blessings,

Mark

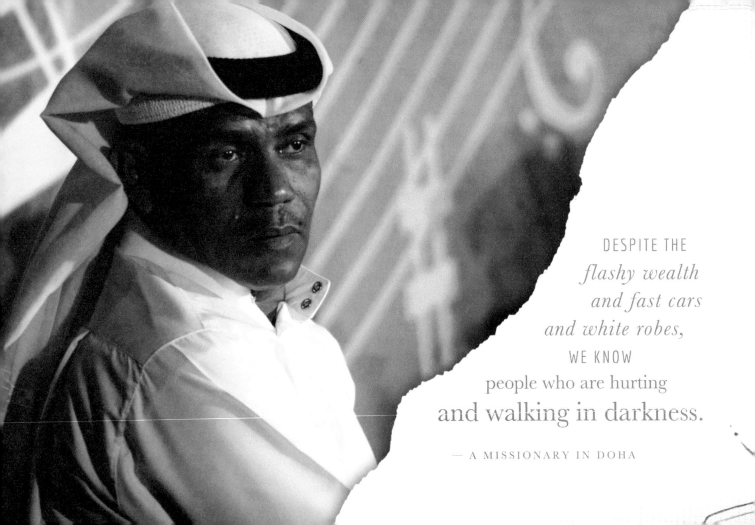

DESPITE THE
flashy wealth
and fast cars
and white robes,
WE KNOW
people who are hurting
and walking in darkness.

— A MISSIONARY IN DOHA

STOP SIX

A Walk Through Doha

A WALK THROUGH DOHA

I walk through the neighborhood, and all I see are walls: imposing ten-foot walls surrounding huge new houses and walls around older rundown homes in need of a fresh coat of white paint. Walls are a common theme in Doha.

The modern history of our country, Qatar, is a short one. Only in the last forty years have people in the villages along the coast moved into city housing. It was then that most of the neighborhoods, like this one, took off. Today the neighborhoods are still changing, much to the chagrin of the locals, who feel totally surrounded by expatriates.

The world resides in this Doha neighborhood: the poor, single men from Southeast Asia living ten to a room, the Southeast Asian families living three families to a house, the professional Filipinos sharing rooms, the Arab families from other countries in humble apartments like back home, the middle-class locals living comfortably in walled houses with extended family, and the wealthy locals in the large walled palaces with beautiful green gardens. Doha covers the spectrum of nationalities and societal classes.

I continue in the direction of the neighborhood mosque. The large local families inhabit the newer homes I pass; the multiple SUVs parked out front are a dead giveaway. I see older homes divided into multiple living spaces, including tents in the yard, for the workers from Southeast Asia who cannot afford the high rent. The smell of their Indian and Asian food makes its way to me on the street. I approach the mosque, a somewhat humble structure and the focal point of the neighborhood, where the men go to pray. It has not been as well maintained as some of the houses; it has chipped paint and a crack in the cement of the minaret.

Looking around, I see almost no one else on the street, which sounds odd but is pretty normal. Families are very private, and women are seen as little as possible. I hear children playing behind the walls and some men chatting. Always there is the sound of construction, and I know the call to evening prayer will come soon. With the call to prayer, men will stream out from behind the walls and make their way to the mosque. They don't stop to talk to each other, though I know later on, around nine o'clock, they will head to majlis, a tent in the area where they will sit and talk until late with relatives or a friend who stops by to say hello.

I met one of my own friends at a coffee shop earlier this afternoon. Our families met at the park some time ago, and our friendship formed over a mutual desire to speak each other's language. We get together from time to time to catch up on each other's lives. One interesting thing I've noticed about my friend and his family is the amount of time they spend together. He and his wife and kids often lunch together and take trips to the park; we even ran into them the other day in a parking lot as they headed to the mall. They act very much like my own family.

What makes this so unique is that according to their tradition, the greater responsibility is to one's extended family—to brothers and sisters, cousins, aunts and uncles, and so on. Much less time is spent with immediate family. Many nuclear families only see each other on Friday, when the man will spend time with his wife and kids. Instead, families here keep a tight social schedule dedicated to extended family—women with their aunts and sisters, men with uncles and grandfathers, and kids with cousins.

My friend does fall very much in line with tradition in other areas. For one, they strictly separate by male and female during any visitation or mixed gathering. When they invite us over, the men are in a separate room from the women at all times—even if it's our full families visiting. We enter through two different sides of the house, and when the visit is over, my wife and I call each other on our cell phones and meet at the car.

And there's the evening call to prayer. As I watch the men emerge from behind the walls, I think about how each person in the neighborhood is precious to Jesus. Oftentimes walking through the neighborhood, my wife and I are overwhelmed about where to start. As I pray and think about each house, I ask that the Kingdom of God would extend to each one, that the Word of God would be studied in each one, and that Christ's freedom would be experienced by the many hurting in each one.

Each house, each family, each person has a façade. Women are covered. The men are in robes. Houses are hidden. Everyone gives off the air that they are okay, that everything is fine. And everything is white—white cars, white clothes, white houses—giving the appearance that everything and everyone in Doha is clean. We know it's not. My wife and I know that everything is not okay; we know people with tragic stories, with hurts and needs. Despite the flashy wealth and fast cars and white robes, we know people who are hurting and walking in darkness.

Despite the walls and the façades, my wife and I choose to look at this neighborhood with eyes of hope. Some days it's not an easy task, but we do it. Because we know that we serve a Lord who wants to send light into these settings. The reality is that there is no way for us to get behind these ten-foot walls, but the spiritual reality is that we serve the Lord who breaks down spiritual walls. The physical and spiritual walls might be meant to keep us out, but we see God helping to open the doors, and we continue to pray for freedom for these people.

MEDITATIONS

Do you know anyone who is hiding behind "fast cars and white robes"? How can you help these people to break down their walls and grow spiritually?

_____

_____

_____

_____

What kind of "ten-foot walls" do you need God to help you break down in your own life?

_____

_____

_____

_____

JOURNALING

1) In this story, the author shares that in Doha some hide "behind fast cars and white robes." Your challenge today is to ask yourself, "What am I hiding behind?"

2) Draw a wall across your page. On your wall, write three things that you might be hiding behind.

3) On the other side of the wall, write the initials of three people you know who need to hear the message of Jesus.

4) Are the things you are hiding behind holding you back from sharing with them?

5) Say a prayer for each person and for each item on your wall. Ask God to help you break down the walls in your own life as you abide in Him.

STOP SEVEN

The Value of Partnering

EXTRAVAGANT DAILY TIME WITH JESUS

BY JEFF GRIFFIN

My daily time with Jesus involves about an hour and a half of Bible study and prayer over a cup of coffee at the start of each day. Well, actually two cups!

BIBLE STUDY

I have trouble just reading the Bible—I tend to fall asleep. So most of my Bible study involves copying out Scriptures, a habit I was taught the day after I surrendered my life to Christ, during my first year at university. A former student who was back on a visit took me under his wing and taught me how to use a concordance and look up verses on a particular topic and to copy them out by hand in a notebook. Later, I was taught how to do a sentence flow chart to understand the thought flow of a passage and how to study whole books. But the practice of writing out Scriptures has stayed with me to this day. It enables me to meditate on the verses in a way that reading does not, and draw out the truths from God's Word.

Occasionally, I will read through the whole Bible using a one-year Bible. This helps me understand Scriptures in their context. Most recently I did this with a one-year Bible arranged chronologically.

To help me draw out the lessons from a passage, I now look for the following. Is there:

- a command for me to obey?
- a promise for me to claim?
- a sin for me to avoid or repent of?
- an example for me to follow (good) or avoid (bad)?
- a truth to believe?
- a prayer to pray?

More recently, for our work with chronological Bible storytelling, we have come across a set of questions that I find useful to study a story: What do we learn about God/Jesus in this story? What do we learn about man? How can we apply this in our lives?

PRAYER

For my prayer time, I like to walk around praying aloud, again to help me stay focused and alert, not falling asleep.

For the first part of my prayer time, I do two things. First, I surrender myself to God, verbally bringing my life as a daily offering to God, and offering myself as a living sacrifice holy and acceptable to God, which is our true spiritual worship (Romans 12:1-2). Another verse I might repeat in doing this is: "Your kingdom come, your will be done in my life as in heaven" (from the Lord's Prayer) and "Not my will, but yours be done" (Luke 22:42).

Second, I pray aloud to take up the full armor of God, listing each item and verses from God's Word that speak about that part of the armor. I found this was necessary to keep on top of my emotions. I name each part of the armor and verses associated with each, personalizing them, for example, with the shield of faith: "The just shall live by faith" (Romans 1:17 NKJV); "We live by faith not by sight" (2 Corinthians 5:7); "Faith is the substance of things hoped for, the evidence of things not seen" (Hebrews 11:1 NKJV); I trust in you with all my heart, I lean not on my own understanding, I acknowledge you in all my ways, and trust that you will direct my paths (Proverbs 3:5-6).

JEFF GRIFFIN

My wife and I have been working among Muslims in North Africa since 1993 and 1997, respectively. We were both sent out as singles and met on the field. We got married in 1998.

I came into this work from a professional background. My father was a commercial flower grower, and when I went to university I studied agriculture. Agriculture is part of me, and when I felt the call to work among Muslims, I wanted to use this training for the Kingdom. So for the past fifteen-plus years, I have been working with farmers in North Africa, teaching them how to improve their yields and at the same time introducing them to Jesus.

My wife is from Latin America and is part of the new workforce coming to the field from that part of the world. She reaches out to women through doing crafts and sharing stories from God's Word, especially the story of God's cosmic plan of salvation through Jesus.

Sometimes for variety I will pray the Lord's Prayer, expanding and personalizing each line. It covers the same areas plus others. Or another prayer I pray, usually for coworkers but also for myself, is Paul's prayer for the Colossians (1:9-12).

Then I have an intercession time with a different focus each day: coworkers, team members, the lost, authorities, national believers, and the church.

Two last things about abiding: I have never been very successful at Scripture memorization. I tried this early on in my Christian walk, but never really picked it up as a habit. But I have found that two habits I have incorporated enable me to memorize Scripture without directly trying. First, the habit of copying out Scriptures naturally indents significant verses in my memory. Second, praying Scriptures and quoting them in my prayers regularly does the same thing. The objective is different—to use the Scriptures in praying—but the result is the same: Scripture memorization.

Last, God revolutionized my devotional time in 1998 when, along with a challenge to begin fasting and praying for our area, He asked me to give up my Saturday take-it-easy morning. Until that time, I prayed and read my Bible each day, but Saturday was always a day I left for sleeping in a little. I would read my Bible quickly and skip prayer. God put His finger on that and said: "I want you to give me every day, including Saturday." That transformed my devotional times with Jesus. I became far more disciplined.

MEDITATIONS

What can you do to make your spiritual life and prayer time more disciplined?

_____

_____

_____

_____

_____

What do you think God is putting His finger on in your life that you should eliminate to be more spiritually disciplined?

_____

_____

_____

_____

JOURNALING

1) List five things you need to cut out of your schedule so that you can become more spiritually disciplined.

_____

_____

_____

2) Optional: Use markers or paint to illustrate what your life could look like if freed from life's tight schedules. (Remember, there is no wrong or right to this exercise.)

WE CAN'T DO IT ALONE

BY JEFF GRIFFIN

Two are better than one because they have a good return for their work: If one falls down, his friend can help him up. But pity the man who falls and has no one to help him up. . . . Though one may be overpowered, two can defend themselves. A cord of three strands is not quickly broken. —ECCLESIASTES 4:9-12 (NIV 84)

The rationale for partnering is simple: We can't do it alone. Everywhere in the Arab world, there are so many who are unreached and so few workers. The task is so huge that we can't do it alone—we need to work together to accomplish the task. This means partnering with each other, just as Jesus sent His disciples out in pairs (Mark 6:7).

Partnership occurs on many levels: with God, coworkers, and other agencies and organizations. Ultimately, it describes our relationship with the national church when it reaches maturity, partnering with them to reach their own people.

One story from our time in North Africa illustrates this. During the course of our project work, we developed a close relationship with one family. In 2004, we began to work on a project to develop a set of Bible stories to share God's plan of salvation with Muslims. We worked with a national believer named Abel to prepare the stories in the local dialect. We then began to visit this family each month to share the stories with them, partly to test them out, partly to proclaim the good news to them. We went through Creation, Adam and Eve, Noah, Abraham, and Moses before coming to Jesus. The children loved the stories, and we learned later that the oldest daughter began to believe during this time.

Later, a coworker visited the family with Abel. He realized that they already knew a lot, and he challenged the family to follow Christ. The father had allowed us to teach his children but had held back himself. However, when he saw Abel, a national like himself, he got excited and accepted the Lord. Later he and the whole family were baptized, and I can remember the incredible smile of joy on his face after his baptism.

That story illustrates partnership on several levels: with a national worker (Abel) to produce the stories; my wife and me working together to share the stories with the family and lay a solid foundation; and finally Abel and a coworker visiting the family and leading them to Christ.

Partnership occurs on several different levels:

PARTNERSHIP WITH GOD

When my wife and I moved to the interior of North Africa to work among farmers in 1998, we struggled to find our bearings throughout our first year. I had already spent two years in the capital, but life in this small city was different. In March 1999, we attended a conference where we were challenged to believe God for a breakthrough in our areas.

A story that we took inspiration from and used in our prayers was the story of Joshua and Jericho. Joshua had assumed leadership of the people of Israel after Moses' death. And this was the first city they had to take in possessing the Promised Land. It was a walled city, and you can imagine Joshua going out to survey the city, looking up at the walls, and wondering how on earth they were going to take it.

Then he sees a man standing in front of him with a drawn sword in his hand. Joshua goes up to him and asks, "Are you for us or for our enemies?" The man replies, "Neither, but as commander of the army of the Lord I have now come." He then proceeds to give Joshua instructions on how to take Jericho, rather unconventional instructions: marching around the city once each day for six days, then on the seventh day marching around seven times, blowing their trumpets, and giving a loud shout. Joshua and the Israelites followed these instructions, and when they gave the great shout, the walls collapsed and they went in and took the city.

We began to pray: "Jesus, you are our captain. Show us your strategy for how to plant your church in this place." Another prayer we prayed was: "God, unless you build the house, we labor in vain" (Psalm 127:1). The answer came through loud and clear during that conference: fast and pray. So we went back to our city and began to do this, fasting one day each week and going on three-day fasts every three or four months.

In April, some national believers visited us from the capital city to follow up on Bible-correspondence-course contacts in our city. I had tried to do this previously but found that it was too high profile and dangerous for me as an expat in our area. So I had invited these national believers to help us. In their first visit, they connected with four contacts who said they were believers. These national believers came back every few months, and each time they located new believers. Not all of the first four were true believers or persevered in their faith. But it was out of these contacts that the first church was birthed. At the end of the year, we were able to look back and stand amazed at how much God had done, all because we had begun to fast and pray.

Jesus is the captain of the army. He is the Good Shepherd. The church is His first of all. And He has the strategies for opening

> The rationale for partnering is simple: We can't do it alone. Everywhere in the Arab world, there are so many who are unreached and so few workers. The task is so huge that we can't do it alone—we need to work together to accomplish the task. — JEFF GRIFFIN

up new areas. So partnership involves partnering with Him first. We need His strategies and His power and anointing. We still need to be faithful in sowing, but it is God who gives the increase, as Paul said about the Corinthian church in 1 Corinthians 3:6: "I planted the seed, Apollos watered it, but God made it grow."

PARTNERSHIP WITH SENDING CHURCHES

"I thank my God every time I remember you. In all my prayers for all of you, I always pray with joy because of your partnership in the gospel from the first day until now" (Philippians 1:3-5).

An important level of partnership is with our supporting churches and prayer partners. Philippians is a thank-you letter from Paul to a church he started, a church that had been actively supporting him and his work all along. Our supporting churches partner with us in giving and in praying for us.

A story from the Old Testament illustrates this. In Exodus 17:8-13, the Amalekites attack the people of Israel. Joshua leads the army out against them, and Moses stays on top of a hill overlooking the battle in spiritual warfare, holding up the staff of God. While his hands are up, the

Israelites prevail; when they are down, the Amalekites prevail. In the end, Moses has to sit on a rock, and Aaron and Hur stand on either side holding up his hands and the staff of God.

There are two partnerships at work here: first, between Joshua and the army fighting the battle and Moses on top of the hill in spiritual warfare for them; and second, between Moses holding up the staff and Aaron and Hur holding up his arms so that the staff remains aloft and the children of Israel prevail in battle. Both can be likened to our prayer partners praying and interceding for us and holding us up in prayer.

Another story from the Old Testament illustrates the partnership between those who go and those who send. In 1 Samuel 30, David and his band of soldiers arrive in Ziklag, their base, to find that the Amalekites have destroyed it and taken all their women and children as captives. They give chase but arrive at a ravine, where 200 of the men are too exhausted to continue. They stay behind guarding the supplies while David and 400 others continue.

After they bring back the women and children, plus a lot of plunder, there is a dispute: Those who continued do not want to share the plunder with those who remained. David intervenes and says, "The share of the man who stayed with the supplies is to be the same as that of him who went down to the battle. All will share alike" (1 Samuel 30:24). David made this a statute and an ordinance for Israel from that day on. Those who send and those who go are in a partnership, and both will share in the reward.

PARTNERING WITH OUR SPOUSES

In the Muslim world, there is a strict separation of the sexes. There are some exceptions, but generally this means that women are going to be reached through women and men through men. That means partnering together. Usually this is separately, but sometimes it can be family to family. My wife and I told Bible stories in several family settings, and we also did picnics with some families.

We also partnered in preparing a series of stories from God's Word for sharing the gospel with Muslims. I did most of the writing of the stories and preparing them with a national believer. But many of the best ideas came from my wife. Then we were both involved in testing them. Some couples work together even more closely, but each couple needs to find its own balance.

MEDITATIONS

If you are married and work with your spouse, how can you partner with him or her in a way that highlights each of your God-given talents and gifts?

If you are single but work closely with someone in your workplace, how can you partner with this person in a way that highlights each of your God-given talents and gifts?

THE VALUE OF PARTNERSHIP

BY JEFF GRIFFIN

First Thessalonians is a letter Paul wrote to a church he had planted but that had been snatched away from him after just three weeks because of great opposition. In his letter, he describes how he was so concerned about them that he tried to go back but was prevented. When he could stand it no longer, he sent his coworker Timothy to check on them. Timothy brought back a report that they were doing surprisingly well. This letter was the result, giving additional teaching to these new believers.

This is an example of partnership with coworkers. Paul did not work alone; he had a band of coworkers who traveled with him. And when he was unable to return himself to visit this church, he had someone he could send in his place. That is the value of partnership.

The most successful team I have been part of never deliberately set out to be a team. We came together around a new church that a coworker had planted and were together for about three years. There were five of us involved: the coworker who started the group with a national believer, a Latino coworker, an older couple, and me.

I was reluctant to get involved initially for fear of expats outnumbering national believers. But I saw that there was a need to develop the worship, and since I played the guitar I got involved and spent the next two years developing this part of the group: putting together a songbook, providing the music, leading worship, and teaching one of the believers to play the guitar. The others

"The harvest is plentiful but the workers are few. Ask the Lord of the harvest, therefore, to send out workers into his harvest field."

— MATTHEW 9:37-38

also had specific roles: the coworker, the national believer, and the Latino worker as the founders of the group, and the older couple who had the best Arabic plus years of wisdom and experience.

We all intentionally worked on training believers to take over, and we all exited one by one. The older couple was the last of our team to leave, after about three and a half years.

The story illustrates the best of partnership, working together for a specific, common goal—planting a church—and each taking different roles and responsibilities, developing these, and then intentionally handing them over to nationals.

PARTNERSHIP WITH WORKERS OF OTHER NATIONALITIES

The task before us in the Muslim world is huge. It is going to take more than Americans and Westerners to get the job done. We need workers from everywhere. One of our teams in North Africa had seven nationalities among its eight members. My wife is part of the growing number of workers from Latin America, but there are also Koreans, Africans, and others.

With different nationalities come cultural differences, and this can make partnership challenging. But other nationalities bring different gifts, experiences, and perspectives to the table. My wife brought an experience of working with humble people with limited education and how to approach this. My ministry experience was with highly educated people, so I was able to learn things from her.

PARTNERSHIP WITH OTHER ORGANIZATIONS AND AGENCIES

Our aid work in North Africa was an example of partnership with other organizations and agencies. Our nongovernmental organization, or NGO, was European and started by workers from another agency. And we ended up as four couples from four different agencies working with the NGO to implement the aid project.

PARTNERSHIP WITH NATIONALS AND THE NATIONAL CHURCH

"The harvest is plentiful but the workers are few. Ask the Lord of the harvest, therefore, to send out workers into his harvest field" (Matthew 9:37-38).

During the year that we saw the church birthed in the mountains, God laid these verses on my heart during a prayer meeting, but with a unique twist. Normally we use this verse to pray for more workers—American and Western workers. I felt God was telling me to pray for national workers. We also sang a song with a similar idea: "Father of creation, unfold your sovereign plan. Raise up a chosen generation, that will march through the land."

We began to pray continually for these two things—national workers and a chosen generation that would march through the land and proclaim the good news. Our vision was not just to plant a church, but a church that would be an army and pick up the responsibility of taking the gospel to their own people.

The traditional view of the relationship between workers and the churches they plant is one that evolves. First it is a parent-baby relationship, the worker having birthed the church and brought it into existence. Then it becomes a parent-child relationship with basic discipling of believers in the church, then a parent-teenager relationship with training and preparing of believers for leadership. Finally, the expat exits, and the relationship becomes one of an adviser and equals in partnership.

In this model, partnership with the national church is the final phase. However, it is actually something that should be done from day one. It is an attitude that we bring to working with believers, and involving them as partners from the beginning is important for the sustainability of the work.

The coworker who birthed the church in the capital city told me once that he followed up several Bible-correspondence-course contacts until he found one that had no ulterior motives and whom he felt he could trust. Then he began to work with him, imparting a vision for the church. They partnered together to start the church. This believer eventually took over as pastor and to this day is one of the key national believers in his nation.

This is a simple step we can easily overlook. We can come to the field so full of vision and passion that we drive the new church plant. Part of the art of church planting is to impart vision to believers so that they drive the church plant, not us. When this happens, we can run with them and it takes off. I saw one church that died after the expat left. He had a national partner pastoring the group, but he was the one driving it. The national partner did not continue in his job after the expat left.

Daniel Sinclair in *A Vision of the Possible* describes a study of church planting in the Muslim world where churches had been planted and had gone on to reproduce other churches, becoming a church-planting movement. What they found was that there was a crucial transition point when the new churches began to plant other churches. This happened when the believers came to understand that the task of reaching their people was theirs. Thus they began to own the vision of planting other churches. When this occurred, churches began to plant other churches.[10]

When I first read about this study, I was excited, because that was what we had seen in the capital city. The vision for planting other churches began in 2000, when one of the believers began to think about a city an hour north of where they were. He began to travel there each week and pray for the city, doing prayer walks through it. Then he began to follow up Bible-correspondence-course contacts there, and out of these started a new group.

A few years later, a second believer caught a vision for another city, four hours away. He began to go there every week with his wife and a single girl. Initially they prayed, and then followed up correspondence-course contacts. After about a year, they felt they had a group of contacts they could start a church with.

Our work from day one needs to focus on raising up national workers, a chosen generation who will march through the land and proclaim the good news. This starts with imparting a vision to them, then partnering with them.

MEDITATIONS

Pray that the Lord of the harvest would thrust forth workers into His harvest fields. How are you harvesting your fields? List three examples.

THE PRINCIPLES OF PARTNERSHIP

BY JEFF GRIFFIN

Therefore if you have any encouragement from being united with Christ, if any comfort from his love, if any common sharing in the Spirit, if any tenderness and compassion, then make my joy complete by being like-minded, having the same love, being one in spirit and of one mind. Do nothing out of selfish ambition or vain conceit. Rather, in humility value others above yourselves, not looking to your own interests but each of you to the interests of the others. —PHILIPPIANS 2:1-4

It is interesting that Paul, in his letter to the Philippian church thanking them for their partnership in the gospel, gives these instructions and exhortations, which contain many of the values essential for partnering. Partnering between individuals and between groups, especially expats and nationals, requires unity of purpose. It means agreeing on a common purpose to work together within the partnership. Agreeing on a common purpose means surrendering our own goals and agenda and embracing goals and an agenda that belong to all partners.

There is a sinful attitude that can detract from this: selfish ambition (Philippians 1:12-18). I pray that none of us is guilty of selfish ambition, envy, or rivalry. If we are, we need to repent.

However, a more common pitfall is to arrive on the field with unrealistic expectations and such a strong vision that we come into conflict with coworkers with a different approach. This falls into the category of our "own interests." It is not necessarily a sin, but it does detract from partnering. And what does it say in Philippians? "[I]n humility value others above yourselves, not looking to *your own interests* but each of you to the interests of others" (emphasis added).

This can be hard work. I failed at this on one team. I had such a strong personal vision that I could not embrace a common vision with the rest of the team. Part of the problem was that an alternative vision and strategy that I felt I could support was never articulated. A clear vision and strategy is necessary for partners to feel secure. This helps build a foundation of trust for all parties so that they can bind themselves to the common vision.

In a healthy partnership, both parties need to surrender their own interests to embrace a common vision and strategy. The ideal is valuing others above ourselves and looking to their interests, not just our own.

One of the most common sources of conflict is from unmet expectations. — JEFF GRIFFIN

Attitudes that mark healthy partnerships include humility, love for one another, respect for one another, and valuing one another. All this needs to be based on relationship. Also, it is vital to understand where each person has come from and what expectations he or she brings to the table. One of the most common sources of conflict is from unmet expectations. Sometimes we may not know these exist, but the fire of conflict will eventually bring them into the open.

UNITY WITHIN DIVERSITY: RESPECTING AND VALUING OUR DIFFERENCES

In Romans 12:3-8 and 1 Corinthians 12:12-26, Paul lists some of the principles for working with other members of the body of Christ, whether within a church or between churches. These truths also apply to work on the mission field. The key principles delineated here by Paul are these:

- There are many parts but one body.
- All parts belong to the body.
- Not all parts are the same; there are different parts.
- We all need each other; no part can say to another, "I don't need you."

In partnerships, we need to recognize that we are all part of one body, the body of Christ, that we need each other, but that we are not all the same. Partnership means recognizing that each individual or party brings different strengths and gifts to the table and that each can make a unique contribution. It means valuing the contribution that each party makes, and this applies to team members and national believers alike.

MEDITATIONS, PART ONE

The missionary tells us that "in a healthy partnership, both parties need to surrender their own interests to embrace a common vision and strategy. The ideal is valuing others above ourselves and looking to their interests, not just our own." Think about your own life. How does this apply to you? How do you need to change so that you can grow in partnership and in the Lord?

_____

_____

_____

_____

How do you see yourself partnering with others to spread the gospel in the Arab world?

_____

_____

_____

_____

JOURNALING

1) Use your journal, a pen, and several sticky notes. Ask yourself how you can better surrender your own interests and value others above yourself. Write your answers in your journal.

_____

_____

_____

_____

_____

_____

_____

_____

2) Ask God daily to help you be a better partner to those who need it.

3) Optional: Write the answers to Question 1 on the sticky notes and place them where you will see them often—such as on your mirror or car dashboard.

MEDITATIONS, PART TWO

The writer tells us "one of the most common sources of conflict is from unmet expectations."

List in your journal what unmet expectations you have had (or have) from current partners or partners from the past. Pray that God will help you to better articulate your expectations to those with whom you partner.

IF YOU FOUND A
cure for cancer,
WOULDN'T IT BE
inconceivable
TO HIDE IT FROM
the rest of mankind?
HOW MUCH MORE
inconceivable
TO KEEP SILENT THE
cure from the
*eternal wages
of death?*

— DAVE
DAVIDSON

FAITH JOURNEY

STOP EIGHT

A Walk Through Muscat

A WALK THROUGH MUSCAT

It's early. I wake up with the call to prayer. Like every day. My husband and I get out of bed and join with our own prayers at home. We get the children up, and after breakfast it's time for school. I'm in language school most mornings while my kids are homeschooled, and we all eat lunch together. The city comes to a halt in the afternoons. Businesses close, and people nap or enjoy family time until activity kicks back in around five o'clock. I then put on my black abaya, kandora, pants, and headscarf and venture out to visit my neighbors, accompanied by my children or my husband. My visit lasts about an hour before we walk home and have dinner. We put the kids to bed, sleep, and repeat.

This is life in hot, dusty Muscat, a city that seems more like a village than Oman's largest city and capital, which it is. It's only been in the last decade that roads were paved. There are no skyscrapers, but there is plenty of traffic with crazy drivers. With no trees, all there is to see is desert and rocky mountains situated along the Gulf of Oman. And it's hot, typically around 120 degrees.

Each day might look much the same for me, but that is not to say that life is ever tedious or boring. In fact, I find life here fascinating. My own

MUSCAT

neighborhood is a great example. Our street is sand; there is no pavement. Each time we drive on it, we make our own road as we go. The houses are mud brick and much smaller than what we know in America, yet there could be as many as twenty-plus people living in these multigenerational households. The Omani people have servants, mostly from Pakistan, India, and Afghanistan. We also have Balushi people in our neighborhood. This people group from Pakistan and Iran has lived in Oman for hundreds of years but is considered a lower class by the Omani people. My Omani friends find it strange when I visit a Balushi friend or shake a servant's hand.

This whole thing has been a learning process, especially in my visits with my neighbors. Life is strict for my friends here, and my friends are women only. First and foremost, it is modesty at all costs. It is required to wear the abaya, kandora (a floor-length dress), pants, and headscarf. I got in trouble once for not wearing pants under my kandora; the ladies checked. Many friends wear their headscarves in their home as well. A young man my husband met said that he has never seen his mother's face or hair. It is risky for a woman to show her ankles, wrists, or a wisp of hair. Doing so could ruin her reputation, and her reputation is everything.

The lives of my friends have revolved around finding and keeping a husband. Most of them were married as teenagers, and they now have ten to twelve children. As they aim to keep and please their husbands, beauty is very important to them. They will take any chance to visit the salon, even though the husband will be the only one to see their hair. They are also very religious. They carry counters in their hands to track how many times they say "God." They believe any time they say "praise God," they get points.

I know life sounds stringent for my friends, but the women are very sweet to me. Let me describe my time with them. It is about five o'clock, so I start preparing for my daily visit down the street. I pull out my abaya, kandora, pants, and headscarf, and get dressed. About 5:30, my boys accompany me on the short walk down the sand road to our neighbors. We pass some boys rough-housing in the street and some workers who just stare at me as we pass. This is all very normal to me now. I practice my Arabic and my greetings as we go, and I say a prayer for my visit as I arrive at my friend's house and ring the doorbell. We are ushered into the women's receiving room; there are, of course, no men around.

Women mostly stay in their houses. Their lives are spent entertaining guests, so visits are very formal. I shake my friend's hand and kiss her three times on the cheek and say my greetings. We will keep offering greetings until she stops. As I take a seat, she serves fruits, dates, and coffee. The topic of conversation inevitably turns to children, and I will be asked again if I will have any more. I've gotten used to this question, too. I smile and say "no." When the visit is over, my friend will bring out bakhoor, or incense. She places it under my dress as part of the tradition to smell nice for our husbands. Upon leaving, I share blessings in Arabic: "May God protect you. May God give you long life. May God be gracious to you." This connects with my friend counting mentions of God. My boys walk me home to the end of another day.

Sure, many days might look the same, but opportunities for friendship are not lacking. I have one friend who is in her thirties and, according to tradition, now past the age of marriage. Typically, when a woman turns thirty-two, she is considered "unmarriable" and will live with her parents until they pass, at which point she will live with her brother. But my friend had a different plan placed before her—her parents intended to send her as an Islamic missionary to a country in the West. I drove her to her interview for the assignment and talked her out of it. She is the most religious member of her family and always seeking God. In the past year, she has seen visions of Jesus and has asked to do a Bible study. What lies ahead for her? I am not sure, but I look forward to finding out. It is just such glorious opportunities like this that break up any monotony that we might feel here.

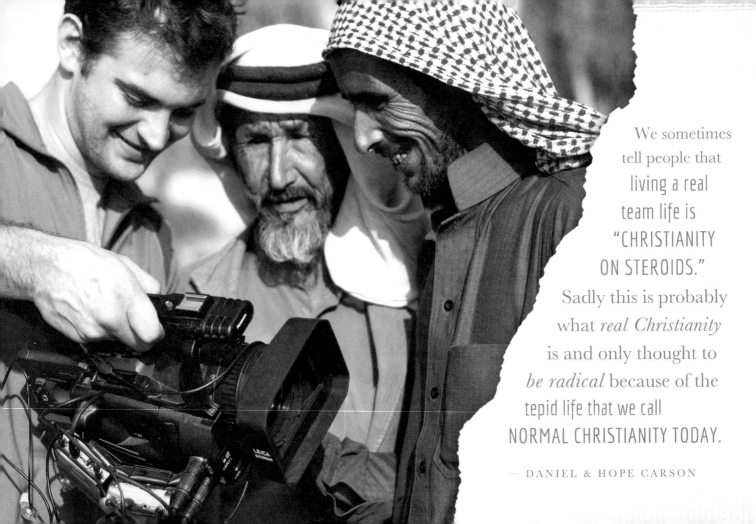

We sometimes tell people that **living a real team life is "CHRISTIANITY ON STEROIDS."** Sadly this is probably what *real Christianity* is and only thought to *be radical* because of the tepid life that we call NORMAL CHRISTIANITY TODAY.

— DANIEL & HOPE CARSON

FAITH JOURNEY

STOP NINE

The Value of Team

119

EXTRAVAGANT DAILY TIME WITH JESUS

BY DANIEL & HOPE CARSON

These are some of our abiding practices:

PRAYER

Daniel: Almost twenty years ago, I made a commitment to the Lord to pray for at least one hour every day. While I cannot say that I have done that every day since then, it has become a habit and part of my daily routine. I spend most of this time in praise and worship, but I also pray for leaders (both governmental and spiritual), my family, our team members, to see signs and wonders performed for the glory of Jesus, relationships to grow with local people, for laborers to be thrust into the harvest, and friends who might be going through difficulties. After I pray for these things, I don't have a lot of personal petitions left.

Hope: As I look back on the years that I've been serving Jesus, it seems that I've been able to maintain an average of two hours a day abiding with Jesus in concentrated "alone time." I love it when I'm able to spend at least one hour in prayer and another hour in Bible study. I usually begin my prayer time by quieting myself in His presence and then offering praises and thanksgiving to Him. I ask God to lead me in my prayer time, and I simply share from my heart. This means that sometimes I intercede more, sometimes I spend more time praising Him, at other times I unburden my heart to my best friend and ask for strength to "press on," and at other times I simply just listen.

However, though this time set aside for "alone time" is vital to me, I do not consider this to be my time of prayer with God. I sincerely work at practicing His presence continually and conversing with my Lord throughout every minute of the day.

BIBLE READING

Daniel: I read through the Bible at least once a year, sometimes using a chronological Bible and sometimes by following a different reading plan. In addition, I love to study the life of our Lord, so I also read through the Gospels two to three times each year. And because I am committed to church planting, I read through the book of Acts every month.

Hope: With the exception of a couple of years when I was trying out different plans, I have been using the same Bible-reading pattern for at least thirty-five years. The plan includes reading the following daily: one chapter from the Law, two chapters from the History books, one chapter from either the Psalms or other Wisdom books, three chapters from the Prophets, one chapter from the Gospels, and one chapter from the Epistles.

SUPPLEMENTAL READING

Daniel: I typically read four or five books at the same time—always devotional or theology books. I am particularly fond of Richard Foster, Gene Edwards, Wang Ming-dao, and Francis Chan. And I almost never go a day without reading at least one chapter of an A. W. Tozer book.

THE THEME OF THE TEAM

BY DANIEL & HOPE CARSON

The Bible rarely uses the word "team," but the concept is woven throughout Scripture. When Jesus was on His missionary journey to bring salvation to the earth, He purposed to accomplish His mission using a team. Luke 6:12-13 says, "It was at this time that [Jesus] went off to the mountain to pray, and He spent the whole night in prayer to God. And when day came, He called His disciples to Him and chose twelve of them, whom He also named as apostles." Notice the kind of team Jesus picked. The members cut across socioeconomic, political, and personality boundaries. These twelve men, with different temperaments and from diverse backgrounds, were the catalyst for the force that changed humankind completely and forever.

WHY TEAMS?

There are many reasons why teamwork is vitally important in church planting. Here we share three of our favorites:

Teams: The Only Biblical Model for Church Planting

Team is the *only* model for church planting in the New Testament. Not only did Jesus call the team of twelve disciples to be close to Himself, but when He did send them out for frontline ministry, He sent them in pairs on two different occasions (see Matthew 6:7 and Luke 10:1). And in Acts 13:2, the Holy Spirit called Paul and Barnabas as a team.

Later, when Paul and Barnabas were ready to go out again, they had a disagreement, recorded in Acts 15:36-41: "Paul said to Barnabas, 'Let us return and visit the brethren in every city in which we proclaimed the word of the Lord and see how they are.' Barnabas wanted to take John, called Mark, along with them also. But Paul kept insisting that they should not take him along who had deserted them in Pamphylia and had not gone with them to the work. And there occurred such a sharp disagreement that they separated from one another, and Barnabas took Mark with him and sailed away to Cyprus. But Paul chose Silas and left, being committed by the brethren to the grace of the Lord."

It's important to note that this discussion was not about whether to do the work alone or in a team, but whom to take along. Evidently, it never entered their minds to take on the missionary effort alone. In fact, there is not one New Testament example of anyone going about that task by himself. According to the New Testament, the church-planting task is always a team effort.

Teams: The Most Effective Way to Get Things Done

Someone once said, "It is teamwork that enables common men to do uncommon things." It is certainly an uncommon

DANIEL & HOPE CARSON

We have been in full-time ministry for more than thirty-two years as ministers of music, as street evangelists, and as missionaries in China for twenty years working as evangelists, as church planters, in orphanages, and with Teen Challenge. We currently serve on the Arabian Peninsula. Daniel holds B.A. degrees in pastoral ministry and music education, along with an M.B.A. and a Ph.D. degree in business.

In our family, we have always operated as a team. Though our three sons are now wonderful men with fantastic wives, we continue to be a family that fully supports each other with our cares, concerns, and endeavors. The boys will tell you that though their father was undeniably the head of the household, all members of the family shared in family decision making and had their voices heard before a final decision was made. We worshipped together and reached people together (the boys often helped with our "English corners" and teaching responsibilities), and we had a blast making orphanage visits as a family. We continue to operate our marriage and team in a way that puts the needs of others in front of our own, while working in cooperation with each other to serve.

(even supernatural) thing to plant churches among people groups that do not want to receive the message of Jesus. The combined spiritual gifts, skills, knowledge, and anointing among team members supply a broad and multifaceted attack against the darkness.

An effective team will function as a healthy body. The parts of the body are separate and different, but they all have their function and use. The body cannot function to its fullest without every member playing its part. Paul writes in Ephesians 4:11-16 about how the body—the team—is built up, becomes mature, and carries out "the work of service."

The work of church planting in hostile fields is difficult. But a mature body (team) with many strong members and with many gifts has a much greater chance for effectiveness than even the most qualified "lone ranger."

Teams: The Best Incubator for Personal Growth in Fellowship, Connectedness, and Community

It's hard to imagine a better situation for true Christian fellowship than in a church-planting team on foreign soil among people groups that are hostile to the message of Jesus. Sheer common interest and need in a foreign culture bring a sense of unity rarely seen in other situations. The out-and-out busyness, noise, and distractions of life at home seem to tear us away from community and make establishing real connections difficult.

We have never experienced fellowship anywhere and at any time more than with our teams as we have labored to plant churches together. Our common interest and shared task help make it much easier to form deep bonds of love and fellowship with each other on the team and with nationals than in our "normal" lives in our countries of origin.

Over the years, our teams have experienced deep love for each other as we have worked, played, and suffered hardships together. Weekly prayer meetings and trips to minister at orphanages have united our hearts and spirits. We have shared each other's Christmas traditions. And even trips to the hospital for broken ankles and stitches have helped create unity among the team.

Our current team worked together to forge a document to express our common task and commitment to team and each other. In it we say, "We will intentionally place ourselves in community, knowing that we have been placed into a body of believers that need each other to be effective in ministry. As a team, we will endeavor to model unity and self-sacrificial love to the church-planting movement (John 13:34-35; 1 John 3:16)."

MEDITATIONS

List an example of how you accomplish goals in a more productive way when you instill teamwork into your work and life.

_____

_____

_____

_____

Meditate on the example above, and write what you personally need to improve upon when working with a team. Be honest and humble about what you need to change, and ask God to help you with this.

_____

_____

_____

_____

_____

THE EXTREME OF THE TEAM

BY DANIEL & HOPE CARSON

Two are better than one because they have a good return for their labor. For if either of them falls, the one will lift up his companion. But woe to the one who falls when there is not another to lift him up. Furthermore, if two lie down together they keep warm, but how can one be warm alone? And if one can overpower him who is alone, two can resist him. A cord of three strands is not quickly torn apart.
—ECCLESIASTES 4:9-10 (NASB)

This passage is often quoted at weddings, but it also speaks to the life of a ministry team. Today we will look at some positive and negative aspects of team. In our experience, working on a team toward a common goal has been one of the most rewarding endeavors of our lives. There are so many positive things to say about working on a team, but we will touch on four advantages that we can see in our passage from Ecclesiastes:

SPIRITUAL UNITY

God did not design the spiritual life of a believer to be pursued alone. The writer of Hebrews says it powerfully: "Let us hold fast the confession of our hope without wavering, for He who promised is faithful; and let us consider how to stimulate one another to love and good deeds, not forsaking our own assembling together, as is the habit of some, but encouraging one another; and all the more as you see the day drawing near" (10:23-25 NASB).

The author encourages us to do one undertaking by ourselves and three tasks together in a body—or team. Notice the team effort in carrying out these responsibilities.

We were created for this unity. The New Testament uses the Greek word *koinonia* eighteen times to convey the meaning of intimate participation between at least two parties. Sometimes those two parties are God and us, but many times this word refers to our interaction as a body of believers. It means, very simply, "deep fellowship."

A. W. Tozer said, "The word 'fellowship,' in spite of its abuses, is still a beautiful and meaningful word. When rightly understood it means the same as the word 'communion,' that is, the act and condition of sharing together in some common blessing by numbers of persons."[11]

A healthy team will experience *koinonia* just as a healthy family will experience love. In our opinion, this kind of unity and fellowship is formed only through times of extended and deep prayer together. Jesus said in Matthew 18:19-20 (NASB), "Again I say to you, that if two of you agree on earth about anything that they may ask, it shall be done for them by My Father who is in heaven. For where two or three have gathered together in My name, I am there in their midst." When this kind of prayer is shared among believers who are united in *koinonia*, the size of the giants doesn't matter, our faith is built, and as faith builds, "nothing will be impossible to you" (Matthew 17:20 NASB).

> When rightly understood ["fellowship"] means the same as the word "communion," that is, the act and condition of sharing together in some common blessing by numbers of persons.
>
> — A. W. TOZER

CARE FOR THE MEMBERS OF THE TEAM

Some of the most blissful moments we have known in our Christian walk have been the times when team members have laid down "self" for the good of the team in real, devoted care for each other.

The author of Hebrews put it like this: "Remember the prisoners, *as though in prison with them*, and those who are ill-treated, since you yourselves also are in the body" (13:3 NASB, emphasis added). That's what happens on a team—people begin to "walk in each other's shoes" and carry one another's burdens.

This care among team members isn't just so the team members can feel good, but it is a necessary part of team life in reaching a lost world. In *A Vision of the Possible*, Daniel Sinclair writes, "That's another reason we need a team around us. Our lives on the field are hard. We're away from home and from our normal church life. So often we feel like strangers, culturally out of sync and out of touch. We're attempting a humanly impossible task in a sometimes hostile environment."[12]

GROWING TOGETHER

We are always delighted when new team members arrive on the field because, without fail, they come with a dream of radically changing a city or country. We chuckle to ourselves inside when they arrive because although every team member we have ever had over the years has made a contribution to the team and has made a difference for eternity, most would probably share that they have been changed more inside, personally, than they have changed the outside world. Why? Because healthy team life invariably leads to growth in the individual team member.

This happens for several reasons, but two are perhaps the most important. First, there is a spiritual law of sowing and reaping (Galatians 6:7). When one sows the seeds of self-sacrifice, love, commitment, and desire to win the lost, one will reap a bountiful harvest of spiritual growth. Second, people often shine when they break from their traditional role and expectations and step out in faith.

LOVE AMONG THE MEMBERS OF THE TEAM

Many Scriptures are taken out of context, and thus actually, in a way, misquoted. One of our favorite "misquoted" passages is 1 Corinthians 13, the "love chapter." Most of the time when you hear these verses, you are at a wedding and people tear up as they hear "love is patient, love is kind." While Paul's words aptly apply to marriage, the immediate context puts them squarely in the subject of "church relationship" or "body of Christ ministry." Paul was writing about the church (and teams) when he penned these words. Take some time to read this chapter in the light of church-planting teams.

Our current team wrote a document to express our love commitment to each other. It says, in part, "We will establish and maintain trust with one another, encouraging one another, building up one another in love, strengthening the local body we have chosen to join (Philippians 2:1-4)."

SOME NEGATIVE ASPECTS OF TEAM

Wow! All of these wonderful things about team life are so exciting you might be tempted to say, "Who needs heaven?" But this is not the whole story. Teams, after all, are made up of imperfect people, so no team is perfect. Here are three potentially negative aspects of team life:

Amplified Pains

While the close fellowship and *koinonia* of team can be a huge blessing, it also opens us up to amplified hurts.

Sinclair writes, "One can almost smell those pies in the oven during future team meetings on the field!" But he goes on to say, "Though sometimes those expectations are actually fulfilled, reality tells another side of the story: Probably the biggest source of pain on the field for workers is from fellow teammates."[13]

Our greatest joys have come from the sacrificial love and devotion of team members, and our greatest sorrows and hurts have come at the hands of team members. The reality is that when you open your heart to love someone (as in a team) you also open your heart to have it hurt more if the other person is unkind or unloving. Although in our experience it is rare, it can and does happen.

But the wonderful thing is that even this amplified heartache has redeeming value and can help us grow to be more like Jesus. In Philippians 2:17-18 (NASB), Paul writes, "But even if I am being poured out as a drink offering upon the sacrifice and service of your faith, I rejoice and share my joy with you all. You too, I urge you, rejoice in the same way and share your joy with me." Even though Paul was experiencing pain, he was rejoicing and saw it as an opportunity for himself and for the Philippians to grow in faith and love.

Focus Inward, Not Outward

As in most of life, something good can be wrong if it is in excess. Team love and caring can be that way also. The team must always remember that its goal and purpose is to plant churches, not to focus the bulk of efforts in ministry toward team members. The purpose must always be directed at reaching the lost. *Koinonia* will happen in a healthy team, but only when the team focuses on the task of bringing the gospel to the unreached. Healthy bodies focus outwardly for ministry; sick bodies only focus on themselves.

Team Members Not Living the Team Life

Probably the biggest negative facet of our teams has been individual team members not living in the sacrificial love necessary to make a team work. Sometimes this was because they were not willing to pay the price, and other times it was because they had spiritual or emotional wounds that prevented them from doing so; they were simply unable to live a sacrificial life.

To have a fully functioning church-planting team that can minister to lost people and to each other in a difficult location, there is no room for "self" anything. However, when we have seen team members intentionally work at dying to self, our teams have seemed to be heaven on earth.

It is pretty easy to be "spiritual" if your only duty is to come to a meeting once a week, stare at the back of someone's head for an hour or two, and "get fed." It is a whole other level to live in community on a foreign field, sharing life together, enjoying *koinonia*, and interacting deeply in each other's lives. It's much more difficult to do the latter, but the effort is worth the cost, to be sure.

We sometimes tell people that living a real team life is "Christianity on steroids." Sadly, this is probably what real Christianity is and only thought to be radical because of the tepid life that we call normal Christianity today. You can experience it if you devote your life to being deeply involved in the lives of other believers. Our experience has been that one of the best ways to do that is on a church-planting team in a difficult place.

Live Dead Arab World is about dying to self and living for Jesus. We believe that is best done on a team of radical church planters who are committed to laying their lives down for each other and for a lost world.

MEDITATIONS

The writer says, "Some of the most blissful moments we have known in our Christian walk have been the times when team members have laid down 'self' for the good of the team." If you were working in the Arab world, what do you think you might have to lay down to reach the lost?

_____

_____

_____

_____

How can you begin the process of laying down your "self" today?

_____

_____

_____

_____

JOURNALING

1) List examples of how you have laid down yourself for the team.

_____

_____

_____

_____

2) Write down and memorize a famous quotation or Scripture verse that makes you think of putting others first.

_____

_____

_____

_____

It is teamwork that enables common men to do uncommon things.

— UNKNOWN

THE SCHEME OF THE TEAM

BY DANIEL & HOPE CARSON

Meanwhile, Jesus commands us to go. He has created each of us to take the gospel to the ends of the earth, and I propose that anything less than radical devotion to this purpose is unbiblical Christianity. —FROM *RADICAL* BY DAVID PLATT[14]

Just as radical devotion to fulfilling the Great Commission is necessary to win the world to Jesus, radical devotion to living the team life is the biblical method for accomplishing this task. This only happens through dying to self and by being a person who will live dead. What does it take to build a good team? Paul, in Ephesians 4:1-16, highlights seven areas that are critical to team life and work. Each of these areas must be practiced by every team member for the team to function properly.

RADICAL LOVE FOR THE LOST

"And He gave some as *apostles*, and some as prophets, and some as evangelists, and some as pastors and teachers, *for the equipping of the saints for the work of service . . .*" (Ephesians 4:11-12 NASB, emphasis added).

One of the gifts Paul mentions is the apostolic ministry. This is the main task of the church-planting team and must be the foundation, the focus, and the heartbeat of the team. This task should occupy our minds and hearts throughout the day.

Charles H. Spurgeon said, "If sinners will be damned, at least let them leap to hell over our bodies. And if they will perish, let them perish with our arms around their knees, imploring them to stay. If hell must be filled, at least let it be filled in the teeth of our exertions, and let not one go there unwarned and unprayed for."[15] May a radical passion for the lost burn in our hearts!

LOVE FOR OTHER TEAM MEMBERS

". . . from whom the *whole body* . . . [which] causes the growth of the body for the *building up of itself in love* . . . " (Ephesians 4:16 NASB, emphasis added).

The team must have true *koinonia* love for each other. This can be difficult since Live Dead Arab World teams will often be multinational, multigenerational, and even multiagency. How hard it is sometimes to have true love for our brothers and sisters when we all come from a similar background. How can we do it coming from many backgrounds? But it is critical that we have love for the brothers and sisters on our team.

What kind of churches will we be planting if there is not love among the team members? Matthew 10:24-25 (NASB) says, "A disciple is not above his teacher, nor a slave above his master. It is enough for the disciple that he become like his teacher, and the slave like his master." If we live on an unloving team, we will plant unloving churches.

How will unbelievers be drawn to following Jesus if they don't see love among the brothers and sisters? Why would they even want Christianity if we can't even love each other? The love among team members should be obvious and draw lost people to want to receive and experience the same kind of love.

PROPER TEAM FIT AND VISION

". . . being diligent to preserve the *unity of the Spirit* in the bond of peace . . ." (Ephesians 4:3 NASB, emphasis added).

"Unity of the Spirit" speaks to unity in team direction and focus. This is a critical component in a successful church-planting team. There must be an attitude of partnership among the team members. Even more than that, they must hold to the same team vision and strategy.

An important part of team life is laying down our personal interests for the sake of the team.

— DANIEL &
HOPE CARSON

One of the most difficult team decisions we have made concerned this issue. Our team was focused on evangelism and church planting in a very under-evangelized area. We had a couple on the team who were outstanding team members, fantastic workers, and dear personal friends. In the midst of their term of service, however, this couple began to feel a desire to work in other types of ministries—good ministries, but not evangelism and church planting. They asked if they could continue to be part of our team yet carry on their other ministries. We agonized over the decision because we loved them and hated to lose them as team members. In the end, however, we saw the need to stay focused as a team and asked them to join another team more suited to their vision and focus.

It was a difficult decision, but singleness of purpose trumped our personal feelings and our comfort.

SELF-INTEREST BELOW TEAM INTEREST

". . . with all *humility and gentleness, with patience, showing tolerance for one another in love* . . ." (Ephesians 4:2 NASB, emphasis added).

An important part of team life is laying down our personal interests for the sake of the team. This takes, as Paul says, humility, gentleness, and tolerance. His admonition about humility in Philippians 2:4 (NASB) applies: "Do not merely look out for your own personal interests, but also for the interests of others." A kind of special vision is needed where team members truly believe that the value of the team's success is greater than the value of their own personal interests, and they must be willing to lay down their own interests for the sake of team interests.

In his book *The Five Dysfunctions of a Team,* Patrick Lencioni aptly states that often "people [tend] to focus on enhancing their own positions or career prospects at the expense of their team. Though all human beings have an innate tendency toward self-preservation, a *functional team must make the collective results of the group more important to each individual than individual members' goals*" (emphasis added).[16]

TRUST AMONG TEAM MEMBERS

". . . until we all attain . . . to a *mature man,* to the measure of the stature which belongs to the fullness of Christ . . . from whom the whole body, *being fitted and held together by what every joint supplies,* according to the proper working of *each individual part . . .*" (Ephesians 4:13-16 NASB, emphasis added).

Paul, as he often does, uses a picture of a body to illustrate what the church, or team, should be like. He says that each part supplies what is needed for the whole body to be mature and functioning. This takes trust among the team members.

A big part of trust is being vulnerable and having confidence that our weaknesses will not be used against us. It's been said that trust is the emotional glue that binds a team together. In our teams, we are deliberate in communicating that members can and should be free to share anything they need to share—especially during times of prayer—without fear that it will later be used against them. The bond that grows out of "spilling our guts" with each other and knowing that it will not go beyond the circle of our team is both freeing and empowering. That kind of freedom and self-disclosure brings a unity that is rarely experienced by many people, even in Christian circles.

Good teams work at building trust, and good team members work at protecting that trust and allowing it to grow.

IDEOLOGICAL CONFLICT

". . . *but speaking the truth in love . . .*" (Ephesians 4:15 NASB, emphasis added).

At first blush, it might seem that a team devoid of conflict is a healthy team. Most people dislike conflict and try to avoid it. So if there is no conflict, then it's a great team, right? Wrong! A team without conflict is a sick team.

Why? Because whenever there is more than one person involved, there will be a difference of opinion of some kind. Sick teams cover up that conflict and bury it. Healthy teams confront it and work through it.

To be certain, there is a healthy kind of conflict and a pathological kind of clash. The diseased conflict will center on personalities and feelings. Beneficial conflict will concentrate on ideas, principles, and methods. Sick conflict will be about political agenda, and healthy conflict will concentrate on producing a result.

In a team, everyone is usually aware of any issues under the surface, and ignoring the problem only produces distrust and inhibits communication. Teammates must feel they are in a safe place and can offer suggestions or criticism freely.

UNITY IN THE TEAM

"There is *one body and one Spirit*, just as also you were called in *one hope* of your calling; *one Lord, one faith, one baptism, one God and Father of all* who is over all and through all and in all. . . . [T]o the building up of the body of Christ; *until we all attain to the unity of the faith* . . ." (Ephesians 4:4-6, 13 NASB, emphasis added).

When our task is an eternal one—such as winning souls and planting a church where none exists—we need to see a victory. The stakes are too high to fail. "Unity and victory are synonymous," says Samora Machel. Paul says we have one body, Spirit, hope, Lord, faith, baptism, God, and Father. That sounds a lot like unity to us.

How does unity in a team develop and grow? Beside some of the things we have already mentioned, there are a couple of things we should do and some that we should not. Let's talk about the negative first. James 3:16 (NASB) tells us that "where jealousy and selfish ambition exist, there is disorder and every evil thing." A healthy team will be able to minimize jealousy and selfish ambition.

In the next verse, James gives us the positive side of unity when he says, "The wisdom from above is first pure, then peaceable, gentle, reasonable, full of mercy and good fruits, unwavering, without hypocrisy" (3:17 NASB). No problem, right? Oh wait, we also need to share what we have (2 Corinthians 8), be partners in ministry (Galatians 2:9), make a commitment to each other (Philippians 1:5), and walk in honesty (1 John 1:6). We don't know about you, but we are feeling a bit overwhelmed at this point. How can we do all of these things?

The good news is that all of these will be taken care of if we do but one thing: die. Live dead. If we can take care of that, it will work. But wait, we can't even do that. Okay, we have to let the Holy Spirit accomplish that in us. Our duty is to die daily and let the Spirit live through us. Then we will be able to walk in unity.

Daniel Sinclair offers this advice: "[This] calls [for] accepting one another (Romans 15:7) and showing tolerance for one another in love (Ephesians 4:2). None of us . . . has 'arrived' yet. We all have sins, habits, and ways of communicating or doing things that are irritating or offensive to our fellow workers. Get used to it!"[17]

Serving on a church-planting team where there is no church is hard work, yes, but so overwhelmingly exciting that every small ambition we can think of pales in comparison.

Oswald J. Smith put it like this: "You can do what millions of others have done if you want to. You can settle for the monotony of American life, get married, raise children, work, retire, die, and be forgotten, or . . . you can become a pioneer. A trailblazer. Invest your life in great adventure for God, and be the first to give some unreached tribe the gospel, and be remembered forever. Which is it to be? It is for you to decide."[18]

Are you ready to join a real team? Are you ready to push back the darkness and help plant a church where there is none? It starts with death. Our challenge: Live dead!

MEDITATIONS

If you are working in any kind of a team environment, what roadblocks hold you back from being a trailblazer for God?

_____

_____

_____

_____

Pray that God will show you how you can smooth out roadblocks holding you back from being the trailblazer He wants you to be.

_____

_____

_____

_____

_____

JOURNALING

1) Find a magazine and colored pen.

2) Reflect on the tremendous amount of unity a band needs to stay in rhythm together.

3) Think of a song by your favorite band, and write down the chorus.

4) Tear images from the magazine that remind you of the word rhythm, and place or tape them near the chorus.

5) Pray that God's rhythm would flow in your life and in the Muslim world.

STOP TEN

The Role of the Holy Spirit in Maintaining a Soft Heart in Hard Places

THE ROLE OF THE HOLY SPIRIT IN MAINTAINING A SOFT HEART IN HARD PLACES

BY MARK RENFROE

Christie has been part of a Live Dead Arab World church-planting team for six months. She is frustrated by the aggressiveness she experiences every day on the streets of her city. It appears that she is becoming increasingly negative toward her husband, colleagues, and about life in the Arab world. The excitement she had when she arrived on the field is long gone, and she's wondering if she can make it.

Dear Christie,

I have lived in the Arab world for twenty years, and I still face some of the frustrations you feel. The traffic, the aggressive way people push, the extreme noise of an urban setting, and the outward piety of my neighbors that doesn't seem to affect their behavior wear on me. I get frustrated by the way men look at my wife, daughter, sisters in the faith, and other women on the street. If I'm not careful, I can become cynical and angry, and when that happens, the devil wins. Too much is at stake for me to let that happen. Let me share with you what I do when I see those attitudes and actions creeping up in my life.

The first thing I do is to take the smile test. I know it sounds cheesy, but I simply look in the mirror to see what my face looks like. Is my face soft or hard? When was the last time I laughed at life and at myself? Am I having fun anymore? These may sound like superficial questions, but the one thing I have discovered over the years is that the singular thing people have in common when they decide to leave the field is that they have lost their joy.

I love Galatians 5. In the latter part of the chapter, Paul talks about the "works" of the flesh and the "fruit" of the Spirit. There are no believers in my neighborhood (at least not yet, but we're believing that this will soon change!). Everyone is a Muslim. They are all trying to work their way to heaven. What do you think this produces? It produces the behaviors Paul writes about—impurity, hatred and discord, jealousy, fits of rage, selfish ambition, and dissension, to name a few. Here's the reality. Lost people act like lost people, and the more separated they are from the influence of the Kingdom of God, the more their actions and attitudes deteriorate.

What I have noticed about myself is that I get frustrated and angry when I focus on behaviors. It is then that I need to remind myself that Jesus came into the world to save sinners—not to simply clean up their behavior. Jesus is in the heart-transplant business, and sometimes I need to ask Him to work on mine so that I can lead others to Him.

Galatians 5:22 tells us that the "fruit" of the Holy Spirit is love, joy, peace, kindness, gentleness, etc. Fruit is the opposite of works. Living in the presence of Jesus will produce these qualities in me. Yes, that will make me look very different to my neighbors, but for all the right reasons. When I'm living close to Jesus, the Holy Spirit works like a magnet in me. He restores my joy. And who doesn't want to be around joyful people?

Christie, the naiveté you brought to the field is long gone. The question is what will replace it. Will you live daily in the light of the Father and become the spiritual magnet that He desires you to be? Or will you let cynicism and anger take root? As you have discovered, it isn't our love for the lost that sustains us, it's the Father's love for us. I'm confident that you will find your joy renewed and your first love restored as you move toward Him.

Your fellow pilgrim,

I don't wake up
in the morning
feeling apostolic.
BUT THE SHEER WEIGHT OF A
glorious, living God
who loves each one
of these millions He
uniquely created
COMPELS ME TO RESPOND.

— ALAN JOHNSON

STOP ELEVEN

The Value of Apostolic Function

EXTRAVAGANT DAILY TIME WITH JESUS

BY ALAN JOHNSON

I became a believer at age seventeen and felt a call to ministry when I was twenty. I thank God that there were people early on in my Christian life who challenged me to a daily time with Jesus. The most important thing in developing my abiding time has been the idea of building diversity into the experience. The illustration that I remember hearing relates to our eating habits. Most of us like ice cream, but if we had to eat ice cream three times a day every day, very soon we would be sick of it. Just as variety is a key in our diets, so it is in developing a devotional life for the long haul. So I have a daily goal—two and a half hours of time with Jesus—but then I think in terms of a week and having certain activities happen in the course of that timeframe. Thus I do not do the same things every day, or even on the same day, but there are core practices and then other occasional activities.

THE CORE PRACTICES

I start my day with sixty to ninety minutes of time focused primarily in Scripture. I usually read three or more Psalms each day, finishing a cycle in about two months. Then I read one chapter of Proverbs a day. I use this reading in Psalms and Proverbs also to focus prayer on things that are on my heart. For instance, I will pray this material for my children and grandchildren, for pastors, and ministry situations I am facing.

I also have a reading schedule so that I read the Old Testament once a year and the New Testament generally four to five times at varying speeds and using different versions. A normal cycle is three months, and then I will do a fast read in one month, perhaps using a version different from the NIV, then another three- or four-month cycle, then a faster one. I find that breaking up the size, speed, and version keeps it from becoming a rote exercise and opens me to new insights.

In this time, I also incorporate memorization and meditation. I choose either a topic (such as the Cross and Resurrection) or a larger unit, a chapter or more, to try to commit to memory but with a greater focus on meditation and thinking about the passage.

I have kept a journal of spiritual insights and prayer for thirty years. I buy a notebook and divide each month into twelve pages. The first page is for current prayer issues, and then on the following eleven pages I make my entries. I do not write every day; sometimes a week will go by without an entry, but I try to stay current on writing out struggles, victories, prayers, and insights that I get from the Word and the Spirit.

This initial time in Scripture and reading is unrushed and integrated with intercession and singing praise, thanksgiving, confession, silence, and so on. I have found that it is critical for me to have a time where I let the Lord speak to me from His Word and by the Spirit about my own issues.

PRAYER AND PRAYER TOOLS

Over the years, I have developed prayer tools that help guide my times of intercession. I normally shoot to have an hour of intercession each day. In addition to my spiritual journal, I have recently incorporated a smaller notebook that I can put in my shirt pocket for ongoing themes and special requests. By days I list missionaries and Christian workers in different parts of the world and pray for them. Then I have themes for Thailand, pastors, Thai Buddhists by name, Thai Muslims by name, all of my extended family members on my wife's side and mine, goals and dreams for the next year and for five years, people I have met while traveling and witnessed to, and so on. I use unreached peoples guides and *Operation World*.[19] I like maps, so I have a map book that helps me focus as I pray for people and peoples around the world.

I have found that sitting for sixty to ninety minutes is about all I can do and retain focus. So I tend to do my intercession times in a more mobile fashion. I love to prayer walk, and I often run and pray as well; it gets me out and away from people and the phone. In a big city, there is a lot of commuting and traffic, so I focus my travel time on intercessory prayer. I don't listen to music or the radio when I'm in traffic but use the time for speaking in tongues and praying, and at the long lights I can consult my prayer guide. This puts prayer and intercession as an activity in chunks throughout the day.

BIBLE STUDY

When I was in Bible school, a professor gave great advice: Never use your personal devotional time for message development. I have always kept that time separate. However, I have found it beneficial to incorporate more detailed study of Scripture into the rhythm of my week. Normally this takes three different expressions. The first is in my memorization and meditation, where I will often work through a passage under consideration. A second is that I pick a good exegetical commentary on a book and work through it slowly once in a week. Then on another day, I will work with exegetical tools and take notes for integration into materials that I file by biblical book and also make explanatory notes in a Bible that I use for that purpose.

SUPPLEMENTAL READING

I have benefited greatly from reading other things maybe once or twice in a week during my devotional time. Generally these have been in two categories: spiritual disciplines and prayer, or biblical theology of mission. I read slowly, mark up these books extensively, and record insights in my spiritual journal. I have found some of the material in the *Book of Common Prayer*[20] to be useful in confession of sin and as prayer themes for intercession.

SECRETS FOR STAYING FRESH

I have done a few things that I feel have kept me fresh over the years. The first is that these practices serve me; they are not a bondage. Richard Foster reminds us that the spiritual disciplines are doors to freedom. There are days when the schedule is crazy and I don't make my goals, but rather than be stressed I just relax and do what I can do. I figure that one day in seven I am only going to get about one hour total of devotional exercise in, and that is okay. If that happens, I come to the next day refreshed and looking forward to having more time in God's presence.

People often ask, *What if you don't want to pray or don't feel like praying?* Many times we are distracted and have so much on our minds that we can't focus. I read some good advice years ago that has helped me so much: Don't fight against the distractions, but integrate them into your prayer. If my mind is jumping to a million things, I might start by sitting quietly and as each distraction comes, I write it down and pray over it. Usually I find that after I have clarified it by writing it down and bringing it before the Lord, I can then focus on reading the Word or praying for others.

A third thing is that we can help ourselves by adding corporate times of prayer to our weekly schedule. This creates a kind of accountability and builds into our schedules times for intercession. I prayer walk two hours on Saturdays with a local church; I go to a church building on Friday nights and spend two hours in prayer with whomever is around; I meet a pastor during the week when possible for an hour of prayer before we talk about work.

For many years, Friday has been my day of fasting and prayer, and more recently with a Thai church we take the last week of the month and fast Wednesday through Friday and have a corporate prayer meeting that Friday night. Blocking out time helps, because even if things are going crazy, you already have this chunk of time in the schedule.

GOING WHERE JESUS IS NOT KNOWN

BY ALAN JOHNSON

When I walk out my door, I am surrounded by millions of people. Most of them are Buddhists, but there are also many Muslims. I walk through slums filled with the most drastic and complex of human problems. And I don't see a line of apostles, megachurch leaders, or Christian superstars waiting to get in and grapple with those realities. I don't wake up in the morning feeling apostolic. But the sheer weight of a glorious, living God who loves each one of these millions He uniquely created, and the compassion of Jesus for multitudes that are harassed and helpless, compels me to respond. So I say, "Here I am, Lord. Use me to take and be your good news in this place. I will take responsibility to do what You ask me to do here."

I have come to call this response *apostolic function*. People get hung up on the word *apostle*, either because they want to call themselves one and take authority over others, or they don't feel like one so they sit on the sidelines waiting for someone they think is better qualified. *Apostolic function* is different. It means that in the face of phenomenal need, the mandate of the Bible, and the burden of the Spirit, we step up and act in an apostolic fashion to go where Jesus is not known. Whether we feel like it or not.

Our world needs literally thousands of new teams of people who will join together, like the early apostolic bands we read about in Acts, to penetrate the final ethnolinguistic groups of our world that have yet to hear and see a relevant rendering of the gospel of Jesus Christ.

If we wait until we feel apostolic, the job will never get done. Are you ready to ask God to use you in this way?

We live in a world that has a shameful division: Large numbers of people have nearly unlimited potential access to the gospel via Christians, churches, and media in their sociocultural setting, while other vast blocs of humanity have either none of these, or have them in very limited number. The sad fact is that today, the vast majority of mission effort—some have estimated it at 97 percent—is misguidedly done among those who have the greatest access to the good news. Mission work has become Christians from one place going to Christians in another place to help them, and tragically neglecting those who have no one in their culture to share and demonstrate the love of Jesus.

The crying need is for people who will step up and be willing, with God's help, to function apostolically—to commit to leading or joining a team that will focus its efforts on bringing the gospel to a people group that currently has no access.

ARE THERE APOSTLES TODAY?

Whenever I talk about apostolic function, one of the issues that always comes up is whether there are apostles today.

Some say yes, and others say no. The easiest way to look at this question is to make a distinction between the office, or position, of apostle and the function. Part of our difficulty with *apostle* has to do with our conceptual tangling of apostles as the

> # The gospel is only good news if it gets there in time.
>
> — CARL F. H. HENRY

initial founders of the church, the unique position of the Twelve, and the fact that the term was applied to a wider group than those who were the original followers of Jesus.

Gordon Fee writes, "Can anything be said in our day about 'apostles'? . . . [O]ne would have to allow that apostles do not exist in the sense that Paul defines his own ministry. But it should also be noted that this might be too narrow a view, based strictly on Paul's own personal experience. His more functional understanding of apostleship would certainly have its modern counterparts in those who found and lead churches in unevangelized areas."[21]

So if we still have the function of apostle in the body of Christ, I think it opens the door both for apostles in the called sense where it is recognized by others as an office in the body of Christ, but also in my idea of functioning in an apostolic fashion in the face of great need. This means that I don't have to feel apostolic when I wake up in the morning, or have some kind of experience like Paul getting knocked off his mount. Those things still happen. God still raises up powerful people in His body to do special things—but that is something God does, and we cannot wait around until those people show up when we are surrounded by people who need to hear the gospel.

I remember years ago reading Matthew 10 and Luke 9 and thinking, *Wow, those guys were really special; I can't do that kind of thing.* But a book on New Testament theology by G. Eldon Ladd helped me to understand the issue of authority, which is a critical component of apostolic function.[22]

Ladd explained that in the choosing of the Twelve, Jesus was explicitly founding the new people of God and that the authority given to the Twelve actually is to the whole people of God. So this means that all of us should be seeking to carry on the ministry of Jesus by His power and authority. We do not need to hold back because of a lack of a dynamic calling experience or signs and wonders in our own ministry. We need to step out in the authority given to the people of God by Jesus Christ.

Don't sit around waiting for an apostle or a big-name figure to show up. Those folks are not interested in going to the hardest places. Get up and start working like an apostle, believe God to use you, claim the authority Jesus gives His people, and trust in God's promises to see fruit for His glory.[23]

APOSTOLIC FUNCTION IN TEN POINTS

BY ALAN JOHNSON

So what do we mean by *apostolic function?* Here's the concept boiled down into ten bullet points:

- God has a redemptive project that embraces the entire universe.

- He calls a people to Himself and uses them in accomplishing that redemptive purpose.

- From the point of view of the individual Christian and local church, there is one task—God's mission or redemptive project—that is expressed in two dimensions: within one's own cultural setting, and outside of it.

- God gives many gifts to His children to use as they serve Him in His redemptive program. The gifts He gives are to be used for His glory and to do His will, not for our benefit or agenda.

- God calls and equips some of His children to cross cultural boundaries to proclaim His good news and plant communities of faith.

- These cross-cultural workers have as a primary focus taking the gospel to people who have the least access; thus they have a different agenda and set of priorities from the local church structures that they came out of.

- Such workers are to function apostolically, planting the church and putting into it apostolic DNA so that it too participates fully in God's mission.

- Apostolic function has nothing to do with feeling like an apostle, but is simply stepping up and asking God to use you in places that do not have the gospel.

- The best vehicle for working in apostolic function is the mobile team or apostolic band in which people of multiple giftings work with one purpose to proclaim Christ to those who have not heard and to plant the church.

- The core competency for all of God's children, whether they work in their own cultural setting or outside of it, is to hear God's voice and obey it.

Mission work has
become Christians
from one place going
to Christians in another
place to help them, and
tragically neglecting
those who have no one
in their culture to share
and demonstrate the
love of Jesus.

— ALAN JOHNSON

MEDITATIONS

Do you wake up most days feeling apostolic? If not, what motivates you to help the lost and spread God's Word on a daily basis?

_____

_____

_____

_____

_____

_____

_____

_____

WHAT DO APOSTLES DO?

BY ALAN JOHNSON

When I started to think about functioning like an apostle, I learned that the term *apostle* brings up a lot of issues. I felt it would be better to set those issues aside and just look at Scripture to see what kinds of things apostles did in their work. Here are the major activities of the early bearers of the Christian message. We can pray that God will use us in these ways as well.

PROCLAIMING THE KINGDOM, BEARING WITNESS TO JESUS, AND PLANTING CHURCHES

Those who were called to be with Jesus were sent out to proclaim the coming of the Kingdom.[24] Jesus then commissioned His followers to make disciples of the *ethne*—nations or ethnolinguistic groups—and to be His witnesses moving from Jerusalem outward to the uttermost parts of the earth.[25]

In the book of Acts, Luke follows the program of Acts 1:8 as the good news moves from Jerusalem and Judea with the establishment of the church there[26] into Samaria through the ministry of Philip[27] and Peter and John as they preach in Samaritan villages on their return to Jerusalem,[28] and then crosses into Gentile communities with Peter[29] and unnamed disciples from Cyprus and Cyrene who plant the church among Greeks at Antioch.[30] Luke then traces the work of Paul as he moves out from the Antioch church to make disciples and establish them as local churches.[31]

TEACHING AND TRAINING

The fact that we have the New Testament is testimony to the apostolic role of teaching and passing the faith on to others. Besides the Gospels, which were either written by apostles or those associated with an apostle, the letters to the churches were written by the apostles Peter, James, John, and Paul in order to strengthen and correct problems in local churches.

Paul traveled back through Syria and Cilicia strengthening the churches[32] and later went through the region of Galatia and Phrygia strengthening the disciples.[33] He casts his own work in terms of being a "teacher of the Gentiles."[34] Paul's instructions to his apostolic legates in Ephesus and Crete involve passing on what they have learned from him to others who can continue to teach it,[35] and to teach what is in accord with sound doctrine.[36] There was a core of material that Paul passed on to his converts and churches that included material from the Old Testament, sayings of Jesus, creeds and hymns, and instructions for Christian living.[37]

MINISTRY WITH POWER, SIGNS, AND WONDERS

It is inherent in the call to follow Jesus that the disciple takes on the task of Jesus and is given power and authority to fulfill that task. Jesus makes the disciples fishers of men.[38] Those called to be with Him are sent out to preach and have authority to cast out demons.[39] And when the twelve and seventy are sent out, they are given power and authority to drive out demons, cure diseases, and proclaim the coming of God's rule.[40] They are called to be in intimate relationship with Jesus, to bear fruit,[41] and to do His works.[42]

In the opening presentations of Acts, the church is founded in Jerusalem and the apostles bear witness to the Resurrection with great power[43] and signs and wonders.[44] Miracles, signs, and wonders are not just the province of the apostles, but happen through others as well.[45] In the ministry of Paul, healings and works of power play a significant role in the advancement of the gospel.[46]

MINISTRY LED BY THE HOLY SPIRIT

F. F. Bruce, in his commentary on Acts, notes that a major theological theme of Luke is the leading of the Spirit.[47] While the record focuses on a few of the key personalities, Luke shows that it is the entire community of followers that is constituted by the Spirit.

Bruce summarizes in this way: "The Christian community is Spirit-filled and Spirit-led, so much so that its voice is the voice of the Spirit . . . and the whole evangelistic enterprise from Jerusalem to Rome is directed by the Spirit."

Bruce points out that it is part of Luke's plan to show that the progress of the faith "was no mere product of human planning, it was directed by divine agency." These "bearers of the New Testament message" were led and empowered by the Spirit to proclaim the good news and demonstrate it with miraculous signs, wonders, and healings.

C. W. Carter, summarizing apostolic methods that were used to make Christ known, includes personal witness, miracles, oral preaching, itineration, charities, church organization and supervision, training of promising converts, planting the gospel in strategic centers, and writing and circulating Christian letters.[48] He points out that this was not simply the work of a few, but that in the early church there was a sense that the responsibility of universal witness was upon every believer. "Whatever social, economic, political, or other implications the gospel may have had, the primary and distinctive aim of the first-century Christians was to make Christ known to all the world as Savior and Lord."[49]

SUFFERING

The ministry of the apostles was marked by opposition, persecution, and suffering. In Jerusalem, Peter and John were apprehended after the healing of the crippled man at the temple gate.[50] They were commanded not to speak or teach in Jesus' name. Later the apostles, as a group, were arrested,[51] miraculously freed by an angel of the Lord,[52] then retaken without force,[53] flogged, and released.[54]

After Paul's conversion, his testimony in Damascus led the Jews to attempt to kill him,[55] and, when he came to Jerusalem, the same thing happened and he was sent off to Tarsus for his safety.[56] At a later period, James was martyred by Herod[57] and Peter was taken with the same intent, but again miraculously delivered.[58] Luke's record of Paul's missionary journeys in Acts is laced with abuse and violence as he proclaimed the message of Jesus.[59] Paul's own letters shed more light on the sufferings he faced[60] and his view that apostles are like men condemned to death, who are the scum of the earth and refuse of the world.[61]

CARING FOR THE WEAK

It is a telling sign of our tendency in the West to split the "spiritual" and "physical/social" domains that our images of apostolic ministry rarely include caring for the weak and marginalized. Our earliest record of the church shows that it devoted itself to apostolic doctrine.[62] Note the concern that no one lack in the new community constituted by the Spirit. While the apostles saw their focus of ministry as the preaching of the Word and prayer, they provided the impetus for the mechanism that cared for the Greek widows. Paul says to the Ephesian elders in Acts 20:34-35: "You yourselves know that these hands of mine have supplied my own needs and the needs of my companions. In everything I did, I showed you that by this kind of hard work we must help the weak, remembering the words the Lord Jesus Himself said: 'It is more blessed to give than to receive.' "

Paul and the apostles in Jerusalem shared a concern for the poor believers there.[63] His work on collecting an offering for them,[64] his concern that widows be cared for by the local church,[65] and his admonition to help the weak (*asthenes*—the same word as in the Acts passage that can refer to economic weakness and poverty in both contexts) show that he did not conduct himself in an either-or fashion. The experience of being reconciled to God, and living as a community under the rule of God, meant that these things were the natural expressions and implications worked out in human relationships of the message that he preached.

HOW DOES APOSTOLIC FUNCTION WORK?

BY ALAN JOHNSON

The first step in apostolic function happens in our hearts, when the burden we receive from the Word and the Spirit in the face of great spiritual need moves us to ask the Lord to use us to make Jesus known. But what does this look like in real-life situations?

In Thailand, where I have worked, the majority of the people are Buddhist, but there is a significant minority population that is Muslim. There are Christians of Buddhist backgrounds but hardly any of Muslim background. Many years ago, I was teaching Thai Bible-school students about world mission, and I talked a good deal about the need for sharing the gospel with the Muslim minority.

Several months later, we visited one of my students at her church in the south where the greatest number of Muslims is located. I asked the pastor, "So what are you doing for evangelism here?" She said they passed out tracts. I asked if they were passing out tracts to Muslims. She said no, so I asked what they were doing. Her response really caught me: She said they would not talk to Muslims at all.

I was shocked. It had not dawned on me as a foreigner that Christians would not do anything at all to engage those around them who did not know Christ. I later discovered that our Thai churches would not even consider doing evangelism among Muslims, but would instead work with tribal peoples that had a greater percentage of Christians than their own Thai people.

ALAN JOHNSON

My wife, Lynette, and I have two daughters who were raised in Thailand and are now married and serving the Lord with their husbands and children. Since 1986 we have lived among the Buddhist people of Thailand and for the last decade have helped the Asia Pacific region to develop a specific focus on unreached people groups that have not traditionally been on our strategic radar. In the last few years, I have begun to focus more ministry time on Muslims in Bangkok; we are building a church-planting team among this group.

When people ask me how I became a missionary, I tell them the short answer is that I was driven insane by a pie chart. Back when I was first entering full-time vocational ministry and still studying in Bible school, I was sent a pie chart that showed the major blocs of unreached peoples in the world. It was the first time I had seen or heard anything like that. Listening to missionaries in my church had never made me want to be one; they all sounded so successful and had revival breaking out. But here was a world of people cut off from the gospel, without any near-neighbor witness. And the call was very clear: Without someone leaving a culture that had the gospel to go to one that did not and plant the church of Jesus Christ, these people would never hear.

Over time, as I looked at that chart on my wall and began to pray, it bore into my spirit until after a period of years I felt like the next step for our family was to obey God and go to an unreached people group.

These experiences helped me to see that as a mission organization we had become blind to the plight of Muslims in our country twice.

First, our commitment to work with the national church means that we are highly involved in filling needed slots for workers that are always in short supply. The result is that other groups, like the Muslims in this case, drop out of our vision. We know they are there, but we are too busy working with the church to do anything about it.

Second, when the national church has prejudice or fear and will not work with another group, the mission team becomes shaped by the national church's agenda, and again unreached groups drop off the strategic radar.

The longer I serve in missions, the more I realize how easy it is to get drawn into all kinds of good activities that keep us from sharing the gospel with people.

Many new cross-cultural workers come with the best of intentions, but soon they are pulled by pressures from the church and mission team to do all kinds of things that move them away from evangelism.

Once while doing a devotional for a group of new missionary candidates, I found myself hunting for words to try to talk about this need to stay on the cutting edge of evangelism. I suddenly blurted out, "You have a God-given right to hang out with lost people!" I followed that with, "Don't let people throw work at you that will ruin your call to reach lost people."

So much of my thinking has been focused on working in this kind of context and trying to find ways to address this problem. Commitment to work with local-church movements is critical in helping them to become fully indigenous. But what do we do when we find ourselves so engaged with the church that does exist—even when it is small and among an unreached people group like the Thai—that we cannot reach out to those who have no witness?

This is what I found myself wrestling with in terms of our structure and philosophy as a mission. This is why I have felt so strongly the need to restore that apostolic vision of taking the gospel to people who have not heard.

The Bible brings us some insight here because of a similar configuration of circumstances that happened in the church at Antioch. The founding of the church is related in Acts 11:19-26. Later, in Acts 13:1-4, we see the leadership team fasting and worshipping the Lord.

Why did this team of teachers and prophets fast and pray? They were steeped in apostolic teaching about God's global purpose for all the nations to come to the obedience of faith. It was the Word of God and the work of the Spirit that made them look outward from their own house-church communities in Antioch to see all of the opportunity that lay culturally and geographically beyond them.

The answer to this problem, given by the Holy Spirit, is significant. He asks Paul and Barnabas to form what Ralph Winter calls a new redemptive structure.[66] This apostolic band that sets out is designed to plant local church communities. Local churches do some things very well, but it is awkward for them to try to tackle tasks that lie culturally and geographically beyond them. By contrast, the mobile apostolic band performs this kind of work much more effectively.

Let's look at some of the verses describing the makeup of this mobile apostolic band and some teams that formed later. What stands out as being an important lesson for us today?

- Acts 13:3-4, 13—Paul and Barnabas are sent out and joined by John Mark, who later leaves them.
- Acts 15:39-41—They break up into two teams: Barnabas with John Mark, and Paul with Silas.
- Acts 16:3—Paul asks Timothy to join them.
- Acts 16:10—The "we" passages start. Luke has joined the team as they go to Macedonia.
- Acts 19:22—On the third missionary journey, two helpers are listed: Timothy and Erastus.
- Acts 19:29—We see Gaius and Aristarchus.
- Acts 20:4—The list of workers includes Sopater, Aristarchus, Secundus, Gaius, Timothy, Tychicus, Trophimus, and Luke.
- Ephesians and Philemon—Paul names several other coworkers.

There are two things that jump out at me in these verses that are often skipped by in favor of more "meaty" passages that are doctrinal in nature. The first is that even though there was spiritual need in Antioch, the Holy Spirit called some to leave there to take the gospel to others outside of that geographic and cultural environment. This means the mission band operated under a different set of values than the local church—which was in keeping with Paul's vision to proclaim Christ where He is not known.

Second, notice that in following Paul's career, Luke gives us an insider's view of all those who joined Paul in his efforts. Thus it is the "band" that functions apostolically, and not simply one individual.

How does this help us with the trap of the double blind that I illustrated above? I see five points:

1. To function in an apostolic manner means that we do what apostles do, and we know from our study here that the cutting edge of that was proclaiming the gospel, developing local communities of faith, building people in discipleship, and

inserting apostolic DNA into these churches. That is the heart of apostolic teaching that focuses on God's plan to bring salvation to all the tribes and tongues of the earth.

2. This happens in the context of a team that is committed to these goals and has the priority of proclaiming Christ where He is not known. This means we have a biblical rationale for not *only* working with the existing church, but following the priorities of the mission band to pioneer.

3. These bands function as teams, and all of the gifts in the body of Christ are needed. (Look at the gifts passages in Romans 12:1-6, 1 Corinthians 12, and Ephesians 4:7-16.) Not everybody does the same thing or is good at the same thing.

4. Anyone who is serving cross-culturally can work in apostolic function by seeking to bring about apostolic goals in any context. This can range from working among Christians doing mission mobilization by helping them to prepare and send their own

The first step in apostolic function happens in our hearts, when the burden we receive from the Word and the Spirit in the face of great spiritual need moves us to ask the Lord to use us to make Jesus known.

— ALAN JOHNSON

missionaries to the unreached, all the way to working in a church-planting team among a people group where there are no Christians. We often refer to the vision of apostolic function as a spiritual genetic modification that gives us a heart for people groups that have not heard or responded to the gospel. It places at the core of every expression of missionary work the goal of proclaiming Christ where He is not known.

5. I see two great needs at this time for those who are considering working in another culture. The first is for thousands of church-planting teams to be formed to do pioneer work among unreached people groups. The demographics are clear; there is a great divide between places and peoples in the world who have church movements and Christians and those who do not. We must make it a priority to plant the church among those who do not have near-neighbor witness.

    The second need concerns those who feel led to work with the church somewhere in the world. They also need to have apostolic function as their self-understanding of what it means to be a missionary and work to achieve apostolic goals among that church movement.

MEDITATIONS

What kinds of unnecessary activities are you getting drawn into that may be prohibiting you from sharing the gospel?

JOURNALING

1) Draw a staircase and think of your biggest dream for the unreached peoples in the Muslim world. Write and/or draw the dream at the top of the stairs.

2) Then fill in each step with the steps you would have to take to help make this dream come true.

3) Pray about the ways in which you can function apostolically in your current circumstance.

Optional: Using markers or paints, color and design each step based on how it makes you feel.

I am His beloved
and as I empty myself
of what clutters my
interior space,
He is there to fill me
AND SATISFY ME,
filling me with joy and power,
through His Holy Spirit.

— MIRIAM SMITH

FAITH JOURNEY

STOP TWELVE

The Value of Transformation

EXTRAVAGANT DAILY TIME WITH JESUS

BY MIRIAM SMITH

My daily behavior reflects what I truly believe. Religious routines that are imposed upon oneself, as opposed to those required by an institution or society, are indicative of the true nature of one's relationship to God. So it is secondary really to talk of a daily routine with Jesus. Rather I would share who He is in my life moment by moment; for out of that relationship flows my daily "religious" actions.

Jesus loves me and is constantly pursuing me, loving me, and working to draw me into Himself. He seeks more than just a close relationship with me; He seeks nothing less than union! I am His beloved and as I empty myself of what clutters my interior space, He is there to fill me and satisfy me, filling me with joy and power, through His Holy Spirit. I want to live aware of His love and pursue it every minute of my life. I want to lay aside anything that takes up space in my heart—His home—and allow Him to fill me to the horizons of my life. I want to have the faith to come to Him as needy as an infant believing that He is all I need and that He desires to give me all He is. When I am afraid of letting go, I open my palms upward and let Him draw my fear into His marvelous love, which is so high and long and wide and deep that I have the privilege of spending my whole life experiencing it, if I will only let Him.

MEDITATIONS

The missionary talks about religious routines and how she would rather share who God is in her life moment by moment, for out of that flows her daily religious actions. Do you find yourself caught up in "religious" routines versus practicing the presence of God all day?

_____

_____

_____

_____

What kind of changes can you make in your daily abiding that would help your practices not seem legalistic?

_____

_____

_____

_____

_____

TRANSFORMATION TO WHAT?

BY MIRIAM SMITH

Transformation is a change from a condition of human existence contrary to God's purposes to one in which people are able to enjoy fullness of life in harmony with God. —*TRANSFORMATION: THE CHURCH IN RESPONSE TO HUMAN NEED,* WHEATON CONSULTATION, 1983

What images come to mind when you think about the word *transformation?* The Bible speaks at length about being transformed. Paul exhorts Roman believers: "Do not conform any longer to the pattern of this world, but be transformed by the renewing of your mind. Then you will be able to test and approve what God's will is—his good, pleasing and perfect will" (Romans 12:2 NIV 84).

All people are bound to the pattern of this world, which refers to the way sin, selfishness, idolatry, domination, and greed play out in various cultures and worldviews. God wants people to be transformed from the sinful, destructive pattern of this world to the harmonious, loving, and just pattern of the Kingdom of God. Only Jesus Christ can break this pattern and truly transform people through renewing their minds. Only truth can renew the minds of people, and truth is found in the Bible.

To bring about transformation in our communities, we must address root attitudes, beliefs, and ultimately worldview—our own worldview and the worldview of those to whom we are ministering. People-centered transformational development provides hundreds of opportunities for God's people to confront the ingrained "patterns of this world" with biblical truth, and it provides people with the best possible vision for the future. Development moves from secular to transformational when people's actions and responses deal with the whole of life and confront the lies of a culture with relevant and appropriate biblical truth during strategically initiated development activities. People are given an opportunity not only to solve physical problems but also to understand, embrace, and live the spiritual dimensions of life offered only in Christ.

Before we try to change people's behaviors, minds, beliefs, or lives, we must know and understand where they are now and give them a vision of something better. This is precisely what the Word of God does as we study it and understand God's wonderful plan of redemption. He gives us a vision of a better future and a better way to live life today.

God has the perfect vision of the future; He knows what fullness of life in harmony with God really looks like! He also knows how sinful, broken, and oppressed the world is. That is why He heard the Israelites' cry when they lived in slavery in Egypt and saved them from their oppression. That is why He sent His only Son to redeem all who believe in Him from captivity to sin and the curse. God's desire is always to redeem, to save, and to bring people back to the way He intended them to live.

Isaiah 1 provides an insight into God's expectations for His people. This chapter describes the rebellion of Judah and Israel. In verses 11-15, God talks about how much He hates the Israelites' way of worship. He says their sacrifices and offerings are not pleasing to Him. What does He want from them? "Learn to do right; seek justice. Defend the oppressed. Take up the cause of the fatherless; plead the case of the widow" (Isaiah 1:17).

Ezekiel 16:49 addresses the people of the city of Sodom, known for their sexual immorality. They are described here as "arrogant, overfed and unconcerned; they did not

help the poor and needy." Out of their many sins, God chose to rebuke the people of Sodom for neglecting the weakest among them. It is clear from the Scriptures that God wants His people to care about justice and righteousness, mercy, compassion, the fatherless and widows, the alien and the poor.

Jesus, the Messiah, is our example. In Himself, Jesus portrayed God's vision of redemption by ministering to people in body, soul, and spirit. We follow His example in life and ministry. Jesus passed on His mission in the world, first to the apostles and then to us, His church.

The Old Testament provides a great example of how a changed worldview can transform an entire people group. The Egyptians had enslaved the Israelites for more than 400 years. Slavery was all they knew and had known for generations. Although they kept their belief in God and prayed for deliverance, they had the mentality and the worldview of slaves. They were used to someone else providing for their basic needs, and they were not used to having to make decisions.

Despite all the miracles that God had performed to free them from Egypt, we see time and time again that the Israelites doubted what God could do for them on their journey. Every time there was a difficulty or obstacle—no water, no food, the Red Sea, physical threats—they cried and complained that they should never have left Egypt. God was miraculously leading them to a new land, and He had promised to make them His nation, yet at times they actually desired to return to slavery!

For forty years, God worked on their worldview. He trained them; He educated them; He taught them how to get along with one another; how to live a healthy life; how to worship Him; and even how to come together as a nation. The mentality of those who originally left Egypt was drastically different from those who finally entered the Promised Land. Israelites, during the forty years of wandering in the desert, had changed. Now they were a team, a nation with pride, able to make decisions, confident in their God, and confident in their ability, through Him, to actually go in and take the Promised Land.

Transformation can happen only when people's spiritual beliefs are confronted and changed. These beliefs are the roots upon which the fruit of that culture thrives. This change should be from the culture's traditional spiritual beliefs to faith in God as the Creator, Savior, and Sustainer of the world. Holistic ministries bring loving Christians into people's daily lives where there are many wonderful opportunities to confront lies with truth in love.

MEDITATIONS

The missionary writes that despite all of God's miracles, the Israelites doubted what He could do for them on their journey. What are you doubting God can do for you on your journey?

_____

_____

_____

_____

_____

_____

_____

MIRIAM SMITH

My husband, Kevin, and I both grew up in Africa as children of missionaries. I was raised in Chad and have spent my life in Africa. As a young teenager, I was called into missions, specifically touched by the unreached Muslim nomads living near me. I studied biology and missions at Houghton College, desiring to return to Africa and work in communities. Later I completed a graduate degree in intercultural studies with a focus on transformational development from Wheaton College. Kevin and I have served God through holistic ministry in Eritrea, Somalia, Djibouti, and Kenya since 1993. We have three children: Katie, Kaleb, and Micah.

JOURNALING

1) Draw a symbol large enough for you to fill with words. Choose one that makes you feel hopeful—a cross, for example, or a heart or a peace sign. Be creative.

2) Inside the symbol, list the doubts you have relating to a personal journey you are taking.

3) Pray that God will help you dismiss all of your fear and doubt so that He can help you be bold in your walk. Pray this prayer for the unreached Muslim peoples in the Arab world.

Optional: Use paints or markers to express yourself by doodling other symbols of hope.

POVERTY

BY MIRIAM SMITH

Poverty is multi-faceted, affecting body, mind, and soul. Therefore our approach should be multi-faceted, alleviating spiritual, emotional, and physical poverty. Each missionary should endeavor to touch and be touched by the lives of the poor. Institutional aid, where necessary, may be adopted but should never replace our personal responsibility to touch, love, and interact with the poor in tangible ways while proclaiming the Word. —LIVE DEAD VALUE: TRANSFORMATION

Author Bryant Myers tells the story of a tribal lady who heard the gospel for the first time. Afterward, in quiet reflection, she said, "I understand your story. I believe it could be true. God might send His Son for a white man. He might even send His Son for a black man. But He would never send His Son for a tribal woman."[67]

Think about the quotation "Poverty is destructive; dignity is the first casualty." What does it mean? What causes people to lose their sense of dignity? What happens to a person when he or she loses a sense of dignity?

Poverty and her hard life and the lies of her culture have made this tribal woman believe that she is unlovable. This type of poverty is spiritual and psychological. Many of the destructive behaviors of poor people come from the belief that they are worthless, and many of them have this kind of damaged self-image. The rich (the non-poor), even church-goers, can contribute to these lies the poor believe about themselves.

Poverty is caused by a complicated interaction of systems that affect every aspect of life: physical, social, economic, cultural, spiritual, and personal. The deepest form of poverty is manifested in the poverty of being, the belief that one is worthless. The poor themselves and the non-poor can believe this.

Matthew records one of the most well-known passages in the Bible concerning the poor (26:6-13). He notes that a lady poured a bottle of expensive perfume on Jesus' head, and he also notes that the disciples were upset: "Why this waste?" they questioned and added, "This perfume could have been sold at a high price and the money given to the poor" (verses 8-9). But Jesus answered them and said, "The poor you will always have with you" (verse 11).

What is your interpretation of these words of Jesus? How does your interpretation affect your actions toward the poor? Who voiced the concern that the perfume was wasted and should have been sold instead (John 12:4-7)?

Jesus knew that Judas wanted the perfume sold so he could take some of the money, not so he could help the poor! Judas wanted to say he would help the poor so his friends would think he was good, but really he was a thief!

Let us look at Matthew's passage more deeply. Jesus was quoting a well-known (to religious Jews) part of the Jewish law found in Deuteronomy 15:7-11. Deuteronomy 15 clearly states God's concern for the poor and His instructions that the poor should be taken care of by the people of God. God says, "There will always be poor people in the land," and that is why He commanded them to share their resources freely with the poor and with other Israelites in need.

As we have seen in Matthew 26, when Jesus said, "The poor you will always have with you," He was actually rebuking the disciples for their greedy hearts.

We should also be aware of Jesus' rebuke to any Christian who believes he or she can ignore the poor or use donations to the poor to enrich him- or herself. The Bible, in hundreds of passages, talks about God's concern for the poor and His desire for justice for the oppressed.

Myers writes, "Fundamentally poverty is a result of relationships that do not work, are not just, harmonious or life-giving."[68] He notes that damaged identity and lack of purpose contribute to poverty all over the world. The non-poor (richer people) also have distorted identities. Non-poor all over the world, from the richest corporate executive to a village chief just slightly richer than his people, are often guilty of trying to "play god" in the lives of the poor. Both have a distorted identity and lost purpose, only it is expressed in different ways.

The poor believe they are helpless and have nothing to contribute. The non-poor believe they have the right to take God's place in people's lives, demanding the right to make decisions for them and expecting respect and payment in return. They act as if their position were for their personal benefit. In contrast, they could use their position to generate wealth for the well-being of the whole community, especially to help the poor free themselves from the web of systems that traps them in poverty. The only way for this to happen is through repentance for the lies and sin that are at the root of all forms of domination.

As Christians, our first response to poverty must be repentance. If we are among the non-poor of a particular societal structure, we ourselves might believe that the poor have nothing worthwhile to offer. We might contribute to the damaged identity of the poor by believing the lies of our society, such as, *The poor should not be included in decision making; they are lazy; they have no good ideas; they have nothing to contribute; they are not clever enough; they are dangerously sick; they are unable to understand.* We may believe that we have the God-ordained right to make decisions for the poor and powerless. We might enjoy the attention we get from "helping" the poor. We might need to confess our pride in trying to be human "messiahs," believing that we can save others with our money or things. If, as non-poor members of the body of Christ, we believe any of these lies, we must repent now.

We must believe that we are, like the poor, created in the image of God, and, like the poor, stewards of all we have been given for the building up of the Kingdom of God.

If we have grown up in poverty and are trapped in it right now, we might believe these lies about ourselves. Again, the biblical response is repentance. If we believe something our culture has taught us concerning poverty and it is not biblical, we must reject it and be transformed in our thinking.

The truth is found in Genesis 1:27, 31 (NIV 84): "So God created man in his own image, in the image of God he created him; male and female he created them. . . . God saw all that he had made, and it was very good." The biblical truth is that every human being—man, woman, and child—is created in the image of God, whole and full of gifts, talents, and abilities. This truth is the basis for human dignity—not money, power, or position. This is the truth that the poor do not know and do not believe. This is also the truth that many non-poor Christians do not act on when they exclude or exploit the poor, as Judas wanted to do.

We are the body of Christ, Jesus' hands and feet in this world. The bride of Christ is the only one on earth fully equipped to work for more just, more harmonious, more life-giving relationships among all people created in God's image. The way to alleviate this kind of poverty is to point people to the true Savior, who alone can give them their true identity and true purpose in life. Through the process of building relationships with the poor, Christians can affirm their value, build their dignity, and help them to see their true identity in Christ. In doing this, we will help to alleviate the deepest kind of poverty. This does not mean that we do not give material things, because people who do not have enough food, clothing, and shelter do need help.

However, let us help in such a way that people are reminded of their importance and value to Almighty God, their true source of dignity. Let us be part of restoring the sense of dignity to the poor, rather than contributing to the lie that they are helpless. Let us give with our hands but force our hearts to remember that we are only stewards of our gifts. Let us humbly acknowledge that Christ alone is the Messiah.

MEDITATIONS

What can you do to show someone who is poor—whether in finances, heart, faith, or another area—that he or she is important and valuable to God?

_____

_____

_____

_____

_____

_____

_____

_____

_____

JOURNALING

1) Meditate on your typical attitudes toward those who are poor.

2) Ask God to reveal to you the attitudes and perceptions you need to repent of. List some of these in your journal.

HOLISTIC WITNESS

BY MIRIAM SMITH

Every activity will be regarded as an opportunity to touch people in love, to speak relevant words of truth pointing them to God, and to experience the supernatural intervention of the Holy Spirit. Within holistic missions, we recognize Jesus' presence and verbally point people to Him, whether undertaking a "spiritual" activity or a "physical" act of compassion. —LIVE DEAD VALUE: TRANSFORMATION

When my husband and I went as missionaries to a northern African country, we were the only Christians in a town of 5,000 Muslim people. There was no church and, as far as we knew, not even one local believer. We were not allowed to evangelize publicly in any way.

But God led us to rent a house that had been destroyed in the war fourteen years earlier. At first, it had no doors, no windows, and no roof to speak of. The people believed the place was cursed, and they were afraid of the evil spirits, the jinn, that lived there because of the people who had died on that property in the war. There was only one tree still alive; everything else had died in the scorching sun. My husband and I walked all around the compound and house, praying and casting out every evil spirit.

As part of our transformational development work, we planted moringa trees, and they began to grow in the terrible soil that resisted every other crop. People who lived near us could not believe the difference in the house and the compound. Where once there had been death, now life was beginning to show! They had expected us to die soon after moving there.

After we had settled into the house, we wanted to celebrate a tradition that the local people called a QariDuqa, a "prayer for the new house." Generally, this is a Muslim tradition that involves reading the Qur'an and killing a sheep, but we wanted to "redeem" this custom and use it as a chance to witness. In accordance with the custom, my husband invited everyone of importance in the district: the governor and the commanders of the army, navy, and police who lived there. We invited the head teachers of the local school that our children attended, the doctors, and the leading businessmen. We even invited the sheikh and imam from the head mosque to come to our house for this meal. Out of respect for their custom, we did not cook the meal ourselves; instead, we had one of the restaurants cater it so our guests would not be afraid of being contaminated.

After eating the meal together, we conducted a little ceremony. We read from Psalm 127:1 (NIV 84): "Unless the LORD builds the house, its builders labor in vain. Unless the LORD watches over the city, the watchmen stand guard in vain." Since they had watched us rebuild the house, we wanted them to know that we attributed our success to God. It was important for them to know from the beginning that we were followers of Isa al Masih (Jesus, the anointed One) and that we submitted our lives to God's Word. It was God who had helped us restore the house and garden to life.

Our government registration in the country was as an international non-governmental organization; so more than likely, they believed that we were infidels who knew nothing about God. We wanted them to know that, even though we were there to help with problems in water, health care, agriculture, and livestock, we did not look first to money or science or technology for the answers. We wanted

Our witness is really not complete unless we incorporate all three aspects—word, deed, and sign—into it.

— MIRIAM SMITH

them to know we trusted God, the Creator, for solutions to common problems. We wanted them to know that we believed God's Word had answers for them. We shared with them from Deuteronomy 28, in which God spells out the blessings of obedience and the curses of disobedience. Famine, sickness, and disease, God says, come on those who do not worship Him and obey His Word. This really made them think; they actually nodded their heads in agreement. It is customary for the imam to read from the Qur'an at this ceremony, but those sitting next to him told him not to read it since we had already read the Word of God.

It had not rained in that area for more than nine months. Poverty cursed the people; they needed rain. As my husband closed the ceremony in prayer, he asked God to bring blessing to the town, and he asked God to give wisdom to the leaders. He also asked God to bless the people and give them abundant life. And then he prayed, "God, give us rain!"

The meal and ceremony were over, and we said our goodbyes and everyone was so happy. We walked our guests to the gate and stood waving goodbye to the men as they walked up the hill. We will never forget the looks on their faces, as that very minute, the heavens opened up and rain began to fall!

God honored His Word and heard the prayers of His people, performing a miracle and confirming His power. That day our witness was holistic. We were able to offer hospitality, serve a meal lovingly, speak the truth of God's Word, and ask God for a sign, which He so graciously provided. It rained for three days, and following that incident people began to call my husband *rob ley*, which means, "the one who has rain." Again, it was extremely important to correct their misunderstanding and verbally point them to God, the one who really holds the rain! Muslims will come to faith in Jesus as their Savior and Healer as we proclaim the gospel with our words, our deeds, and with signs from above!

If we truly believe that all activities of daily life are under the lordship of Christ, there is opportunity during each one to point people to the truth of God. We must look for these divine opportunities to point unbelievers to the reality of the presence of God. Words do need to be spoken in order for people to come to faith in Jesus.

Olivia Muchena rightly observed that "the challenge of holistic ministry is how to live, do, and experience our faith in the development arena. It is how to return the sacred to its rightful place at the center of everyday existence."[69]

Consider the life of Jesus. Most of His ministry happened outside. As He taught, He used illustrations from everyday life: farming, fishing, paying taxes, drawing water, or eating, depending on what He and the people were doing at the time. In the Gospels, we also see Jesus reading a scroll in the synagogue and teaching in the temple. He spent time doing spiritual work in the "church"; however, the majority of His miracles and teaching ministry happened outside of the "church." The Spirit was at work in all of His activities whether He was in the temple or on the street. He always explained the meaning of His miracles and actions. He internalized all the truths of the Kingdom and the Word of God, and He knew the appropriate words to say in each situation in order to challenge and transform people. The words He spoke always pointed people to the truth and challenged their worldviews, beliefs, and values. He wanted people transformed from the inside out.

Jesus always had a clear focus of bringing people into the Kingdom of God, but He was also flexible in His witness and responded to people according to their needs. Someone who is hungry might first be touched with the gospel when a Christian gives him or her food. Someone struggling with demon possession must first be freed from bondage before being able to understand the Scriptures. Many people are curious and like to study and learn; so, they first respond to the gospel of the Kingdom through verbal arguments. Our witness really is not complete unless we incorporate all three aspects—word, deed, and sign—into it.

Whether we begin sharing the gospel by doing good deeds or praying for a powerful sign or sharing a verbal proclamation, the good news message eventually needs to include all three. The gospel message that we present must deal with the spiritual reality of eternal life, but it must also deal with the present, physical realities of poverty, ignorance, disease, political oppression, exploitation, and despair.

Sympathy
IS NO SUBSTITUTE FOR
action.

— DAVID
   LIVINGSTONE

FAITH JOURNEY

STOP THIRTEEN

A Walk Through Benghazi

A WALK THROUGH BENGHAZI

I t was such disturbing news to wake up to: the U.S. ambassador killed in an attack in Benghazi. My early-morning brain could barely figure out what happened, and the footage only showed the same burning cars and people walking through a deserted, burned-out building. The story unfolded, and shock turned to sadness. It has been a year since I walked the streets of Benghazi. Though I had no business at the consulate while there, this attack still punches me in the gut.

I remember our Muslim taxi driver—so generous driving us to markets and housing and government offices, all without charging us. He is so happy to see foreigners in his country after the deposing of Muammar Gaddafi, he does not let us pay.

Typically, Libyans are suspicious, but things seem more open to foreigners. I tell our driver, "I would love to meet your family. Can we go to your house?" He is delighted and takes us straight there. We enter through the courtyard and immediately turn left to a receiving room. A door in the room opens to his

house. He walks to the door and knocks; female relatives peek out. He orders juice and coffee. We remove our shoes and sit on the couch of cushions stretching around the room's walls.

The conversation turns to the war. Our host pulls out his cell phone and passes it around. We watch videos of friends, acquaintances, and complete strangers killed in the war, videos that are as graphic as any R-rated movie made in Hollywood. There is a torso blown off, images of legs with no body, and bloody stumps without limbs. It is so tragic, so disturbing. Now imagine being the person holding this very cell phone, recording these images of body parts that used to be friends.

Here sits a sensitive and kind man traumatized by war. He responds to my questions but in a way that shows he is thoughtful and introspective. I can tell the forty years of Gaddafi's regime and the recent birth pains for freedom, all the tragedy that he witnesses, are difficult for him. My heart goes out to him. How can it not? I recognize in him basic humanity; I can see his deep suffering, for himself and for his people.

At the end of our visit, I ask, "May I pray for you and your family?"

"Sure," he replies as he walks out.

"No—pray with you right now."

He turns around, not knowing what to do. "I never experienced this before," he says. We stand in a circle, and I raise my hands and in Arabic pray a prayer of blessing for his family. I pray for his mind, his heart, and the healing process. The man does not cry, but I can see the emotions on his face. We leave knowing a Muslim Libyan in the heart of Benghazi is very thankful to a follower of Jesus for praying over him and his family.

I did not expect to find such a Libyan. I thought Libyans were rough and tough, but this man, bearded and frowning on the outside, is tender and gentle on the inside, open to friendship and prayer from someone who follows Jesus.

Staring through my own TV screen, I wonder what our taxi driver felt when he heard the news. I see people in the video recording on their own cell phones, and I am tossed back. We push past people in a narrow alleyway lined with shops. I am elbow to elbow with people pressing on me as they go about their business. I see ladies in black abayas, some in headscarves. Pushed along in this stream of people, I look up. Plastic tarps cover us. There are Arab robes alongside Barcelona shirts, hanging from wooden rods. Wooden racks of shoes sit next to tables of purses and bed linens. The sweet smell of a juice stand mixes with the smoke and the smell of grease and meat from the kabob and shawarma stands. On top of that is the occasional perfume of incense to keep the flies off. It is a complete inundation of smells and bodies and stuff.

The Gaddafi regime is in its death throes. The people around me are friendly but cautious. They greet me, even some of the women. The men engage in conversation, much like the taxi driver. We see children playing and friends calling each other. But the city I walk through is 99.9 percent Islamic and has been under the double whammy of political oppression and a demonic system. Every person I am looking at is going to hell.

When I reach the end of the alley, I hear gunfire and see bullets strewn in the road. I look down the street at buildings burned out and destroyed. Physically and spiritually, everything I see is death. I saw pictures on a cell phone of slaughtered friends; now I hear explosions and see walls falling down. Everything, everything around me is indicative of death, destruction.

I feel both a sense of urgency and a sense of tragedy. These beautiful people whom I have met and walked among are in bondage—they need freedom. Even the changes in government happening now are turning against them. As the Islamists come to power, life will become more restrictive. My first thought is the size of the loss, but after meeting the taxi driver, I see a hunger. I have a glimmer of hope.

The city of Benghazi has an incredible history. This eastern part of Libya is the biblical land of Cyrene; Simon who carried Jesus' cross was from there. Centuries of destruction and chains are being redeemed and transformed. The people can be saved, and they will be the new Simons of Cyrene to carry the cross of Jesus.

These beautiful people whom I have met and walked among are in bondage—they need freedom.

We can't pay a price
too high to bring
Muslims to Jesus.
*Jesus did not
hold back for us.*
We will not
hold back for Muslims.
God help us.

— WILL CLEVELAND

FAITH JOURNEY

STOP FOURTEEN

The Value of Sacrifice

EXTRAVAGANT DAILY TIME WITH JESUS

BY AMY CLEVELAND

Mothering is constant. My greatest challenge to extravagant time with Jesus is uninterrupted time alone. I don't have this in bulk. But I need to keep my Lord my Lord. I've had seasons of life where this was a daily rhythm. Every night before bed, with my journal and Bible, I'd go for a walk with the Lord and end up under the stars or at a window alone with the Lord—reading, praying, journaling, dreaming, listening, and memorizing Scripture. Enough time wasn't in lack. I liked the rhythm. I tend toward wanting that again. I recommend it. For me right now, rhythm is something to look forward to.

So in the meantime, my time with Jesus happens less at the same time and in the same way as it used to. Some days it means I get up early and stay up late. Some days I put off chores and lists and take full advantage of my youngest's naptime. I rarely get as long as I want in one shot.

I love to spend time with Jesus in a shower or soaking in the tub. It's private and uninterrupted time. The door is locked and the world is bustling elsewhere. I most likely won't get "Mom . . . ," my cell phone can be elsewhere, nobody cares if I'm loud—singing praise out or crying in prayer or reading my Bible aloud. I get some books and journals a little wet, but it has been a great place for me to be honest and uninhibited with Jesus and still enough to listen. I love to pray and listen outside in the dark in my yard under the stars, and I love to pray in the Spirit at the wheel and sing a new song when I'm driving between errands.

I use a "liturgical-ish" book as a daily guide. I like *Common Prayer*[70] and the Mosaic Bible, with devotional readings lining up with the church calendar. I like leaning into the order laid out and following the suggested Bible readings. I like the little bit of liturgy. I like the cycle.

I journal-pray. I mark up my Bible and highlight the passages that speak to me. I read a little from great followers of Christ past and present—biographies, theology, and poetry. I love Corrie ten Boom, John Piper, Christopher Heuertz, and Calvin Miller. I always am reading something from someone who struggles in a common place of weakness and sin, devoting a chunk of my time with Jesus every day trying to battle these areas. I use hymnals. I also love to get out my paints and create as worship, too.

Let's not kid ourselves that sacrifice is mainly about giving up Facebook and Starbucks.... Jesus died outside the gate like a sacrificial animal, so let's go out there and do the same.

— WILL & AMY CLEVELAND

THE COST OF SACRIFICE

BY WILL & AMY CLEVELAND

Human flourishing depends utterly on a human sacrifice. And by a human sacrifice we mean the bloody death of Jesus Christ. It has always been so. God's holiness meets our sin and demands blood. So let's not kid ourselves that sacrifice is mainly about giving up Facebook and Starbucks. The idea of sacrifice started with God killing animals to cover Adam's and Eve's nakedness (Genesis 3). Then jealous Cain slaughters his brother Abel, whose blood sacrifice was accepted by God (Genesis 4). A cow, a goat, a ram, a dove, and a pigeon all get cut in half so God can make a covenant with Abram (Genesis 15). Abraham walks up the mountain with his son Isaac, ties him on the altar, and raises the sacrificial blade over his head

(Genesis 22). Moses receives the Levitical law requiring daily blood sacrifice amounting to thousands of slaughtered animals each year (Leviticus 1-7). And that's just a sliver of the first three books of the Bible.

Missionary Jim Elliot reflects on Psalm 100, on what it means to be God's sheep:

" 'We are the sheep of His pasture. Enter into His gates with thanksgiving, and into His courts with praise.' And what are sheep doing going into the gate? What is their purpose inside those courts? To bleat melodies and enjoy the company of the flock? No. Those sheep were destined for the altar. Their pasture feeding had been for one purpose, to test them and fatten them for bloody sacrifice. Give Him thanks, then, that you have been counted worthy of His altars. Enter into the work with praise."[71]

Kind of puts a new spin on that cheery church song, "I will enter His gates with thanksgiving in my heart, I will enter His courts with praise . . . "

In Romans 8:36 (ESV), the apostle Paul quotes Psalm 44:22 and says, " 'For your sake we are being killed all the day long; we are regarded as sheep to be slaughtered.' "

All of this culminates in Jesus' death on the cross. In the eyes of the Jews, He was a blasphemer dying for His own sin. In the eyes of the Romans, He was a criminal dying for His crimes. But in the eyes of God and according to the Bible, He was a human blood sacrifice dying for our sin.

And the Bible does not beat around the bush when it invites you to sacrifice. "For the bodies of those animals whose blood is brought into the holy places by the high priest as a sacrifice for sin are burned outside the camp. So Jesus also suffered outside the gate in order to sanctify the people through his own blood. Therefore let us go to him outside the camp and bear the reproach he endured" (Hebrews 13:11-13 ESV).

That's a pretty clear set of connections: Jesus died outside the gate like a sacrificial animal, so let's go out there and do the same.

Our Live Dead value statement for sacrifice says, "We commit ourselves to pay whatever price is necessary." It very well may cost us everything.

REFLECTING THE ONE TRUE SACRIFICE

BY WILL & AMY CLEVELAND

One of the surprising dangers in talking about sacrifice is that we can tend to become self-centered. People who obediently go to hostile environments can be especially susceptible to this. We begin to feel good about ourselves as we think about all the things we are sacrificing to obey Jesus. People who hear of our calling tend to applaud us for our extraordinary obedience. And subtly, on the way to tell others about the glories of Jesus, we end up singing along to the melody of our own praise. We take the idea of sacrifice and turn it into an expression of who we are. But biblical sacrifice was never meant to focus on us; it has always been about God.

Let's not overstate our own value. We exist to point to the infinite worth of Jesus, and specifically to the all-sufficiency of His deadly sacrifice. Listen to the way the author of Hebrews stacks up superlatives about Jesus' bloody death:

- "He has no need, like those high priests, to offer sacrifices daily, first for his own sins and then for those of the people, since he did this once for all when he offered up himself" (Hebrews 7:27 ESV).
- "But when Christ appeared as a high priest of the good things that have come, then through the greater and more perfect tent (not made with hands, that is, not of this creation) he entered once for all into the holy places, not by means of the blood of goats and calves but by means of his own blood, thus securing an eternal redemption" (Hebrews 9:11-12 ESV).
- "But as it is, he has appeared once for all at the end of the ages to put away sin by the sacrifice of himself" (Hebrews 9:26 ESV).

- "But when Christ had offered for all time a single sacrifice for sins, he sat down at the right hand of God, waiting from that time until his enemies should be made a footstool for his feet" (Hebrews 10:12-13 ESV).

Jesus' sacrifice was infinitely better than any before or since.

- It's better because His one-time sacrifice was sufficient for all time.
- It's better because His one-man sacrifice was sufficient for all who trust in it.
- It's better because He presented His sacrifice on the eternal altar in heaven.
- It's better because He gave His own blood.
- It's better because it was sinless blood.
- It's better because it qualified Him to sit down at the right hand of God.
- It's better because it qualifies us to be in the presence of a holy God.

Jesus Himself reminds us of this: "If the world hates you, know that it has hated me before it hated you. If you were of the world, the world would love you as its own; but because you are not of the world, but I chose you out of the world, therefore the world hates you. Remember the word that I said to you: 'A servant is not greater than his master.' If they persecuted me, they will also persecute you" (John 15:18-20 ESV). He says, "Don't be surprised if the world hates you instead of loving you. Don't be surprised if they persecute you. But remember, the suffering your sacrifice leads to is all about me. It's an echo, a reflection of how the world treated me. I am first. I am greater." The kind of sacrifice the Bible commends is the kind that forgets itself in the preeminent gift of Jesus.

And yet in moving toward sacrifice, there is also the possibility of eternal significance. One of the clearest Scriptures about this is Revelation 5:9 (ESV): "Worthy are you to take the scroll and to open its seals, for you were slain, and by your blood you ransomed people for God from every tribe and language and people and nation."

In the place of infinite purity, where all cry "Holy, holy, holy is the Lord," stands a Lamb looking as though it has been slain. This is Jesus. And somehow He looks like a slaughtered animal. Why? Because God is on an eternal publicity campaign. He means

WILL & AMY CLEVELAND

We have been married for thirteen of our fifteen years loving Muslims. We met and married with dreams of launching ourselves into the dark heart of the unreached. Will can always be enticed with a good, juicy slice of theology. Amy has a healthy lust for beauty. Both of us seem to be mesmerized by a gorgeous and raw string of words. Our oldest daughter was our ten-month anniversary present; she loves good books and good friends. Our middle daughter keeps us delighted and grounded with her thoughtfulness. And our young son surprises us with his imagination and perception.

We aren't packing up and shipping out to Somalia to escape an unhappy life in America. We are saying our temporary "goodbyes" here today to voice a louder, "Joy to Somalia! No more let sin and sorrows grow, nor thorns infest the ground. He comes to make His blessing flow, far as the curse is found!" We treasure Jesus among Muslims.

For our family, the idea of sacrifice isn't just a value on paper anymore. We are aware of the horrors that pop into your mind when we say, "We're moving our whole family to Somalia." We are facing them. We are weighing the costs. We are preparing. We are going. It's a mindset of grace, really, that motivates one to embrace a life sacrifice. Simply, we believe that we have sinned and fallen short of the glory of God, like Muslims. We also believe that by the grace of God through the sacrifice and resurrection of Jesus alone, we are saved and given joyful access to God our Creator, like Muslims. We can't pay a price too high to bring Muslims to Jesus. Jesus did not hold back for us. We will not hold back for Muslims. God help us.

for all peoples to know the value of the sacrifice of Jesus. So much so that even in the throne room of heaven God decides to display Jesus as a sacrificed sheep to all who are watching.

Jesus' death on the cross is so valuable that God is constantly working to redisplay it for all the nations. In Colossians 1:24 (ESV), the apostle Paul says, "I am filling up what is lacking in Christ's afflictions." What is lacking? Nothing regarding sufficiency. The only thing lacking is the visible and physical display of those afflictions among all the peoples of the earth.

Don't be surprised that Jesus does not prevent suffering from coming into your life. You may be the image of the cross for those to whom He is sending you. It's not the only thing God wants them to know, but could we ever really overstate its preciousness? Isn't the display of Jesus' sacrifice worth whatever the cost to us? It is. But we often struggle to feel that way, often avoiding the cross He invites us to carry with Him. No one wants to look like a slaughtered lamb.

MEDITATIONS

God uses individuals as His tools to perform good works for Him and the good of all people. Have you taken credit for good works and sacrifices you have performed, versus giving the credit to God?

_____

_____

_____

_____

_____

_____

_____

_____

_____

I have but one candle of life to burn, and I would rather burn it out in a land filled with darkness than in a land flooded with light.

— ION KEITH-FALCONER

JOURNALING

*Tear images out of a magazine that make you think of the word **sacrifice** and place or tape them in your journal.*

EMPOWERED TO SACRIFICE

BY WILL & AMY CLEVELAND

There's an interesting thing that happens to hearts that have the right perspective on sacrifice. They end up saying, "I never made a sacrifice." On December 4, 1857, David Livingstone, the great pioneer missionary, was telling Cambridge University students about his work in Africa. Someone asked him what it was like to leave the "benefits" of England. He answered, "People talk of the sacrifice I have made in spending so much of my life in Africa. . . . Away with the word in such a view, and with such a thought! It is emphatically no sacrifice. Say rather it is a privilege."[72]

How do we get that perspective? By seeing every pain through the lens of eternal joy. "God's primary aim for the human soul is not to set us free from pain in this life, rather, at all costs, to set us free from the comparative emptiness of temporary painlessness so that we can enjoy eternal life." Once again the missionary Paul challenges us: "For this light momentary affliction is preparing us for an eternal weight of glory beyond all comparison, as we look not to the things that are seen but to the things that are unseen. For the things that are seen are transient, but the things that are unseen are eternal" (2 Corinthians 4:17-18 ESV).

Paul learned that from Jesus. Hebrews 12:2-3 (ESV) points us to Jesus, "who for the joy that was set before him endured the cross, despising the shame, and is seated at the right hand of the throne of God. Consider him who endured from sinners such hostility against himself, so that you may not grow weary or fainthearted."

Jesus fixed His eyes on the eternal joy set before Him. We're not saying that having the right perspective makes sacrifice painless. Far from it. The need for endurance is real because the pain is real. But looking to Jesus, our eternal joy, empowers us so that we "may not grow weary or fainthearted."

AN UNPLANNED SACRIFICE

Will's dad died while we were writing this chapter. He died from an extremely rare disease that destroys nerve cells in the brain resulting in a horrific decline of all body and mind functions. He was a missionary in Asia who went from preaching among the unreached and working on his doctorate to eternal paradise in less than three months. He was one of our heroes and was only sixty-four when he died. "Goodbye" to Dad was not a sacrifice we had planned on making.

We were prepared to sacrifice time as a family while we traveled to raise support for the field. We were preparing ourselves to sacrifice some of the comforts of life in America. We were preparing ourselves to face the possibility of suffering and death in a place hostile to missionaries. We were not prepared for Will's dad's death.

It has sobered us. His death caused us to reflect more honestly on our mortality. It's not just a possibility or an empty threat. We feel fresh the real pain of deadly loss.

One morning Will sat at breakfast with his mom. Tears ran down her cheeks as the news about her husband's disease crashed with hurricane force into the quiet morning. She groaned under the weight of the sacrifice. But then a defiant cry rose from her heart and pierced the air: "I would do it all over again. I would raise up a million young people to go to the hard places. I would do it all over again. Jesus, you are worthy." Amen.

JOURNALING

1) Think of somebody who inspires you by the sacrifices he or she makes for others.

2) List the characteristics that make this person so inspirational to you.

3) Use these characteristics to inspire your journal page however you desire.

STOP FIFTEEN

Reflection:
When Daddy Goes to Prison

REFLECTION: WHEN DADDY GOES TO PRISON

BY DICK BROGDEN

Security police arrested a missionary colleague recently, and his family didn't hear from him for days. I was thinking about what I would want someone to tell my boys, Luke and Zack, if I was in prison. Here is what I would want them to know:

1) GOD LOVES AND TRUSTS YOUR DAD ENOUGH TO SEND HIM TO PRISON.

In Mark 1:10, the Holy Spirit descends on Jesus. In Mark 1:11 (ESV), God says, "You are my beloved Son; with you I am well pleased." And then in the very next verse, the Spirit drives Jesus into the wilderness—where angels minister to Him. Your papa is in prison because God loves and trusts him, and God will send angels to minister to your papa.

2) GOD IS COMPLETELY IN CONTROL.

In John 19:10-11 (ESV), Pilate says to Jesus, "Do you not know I have authority to release you and authority to crucify you?" Jesus responds, "You would have no authority over me at all unless it had been given you from above." Governments, police, and security all act really tough and scary, but they have authority only because God has given it. In comparison to God, they are powerless.

God could destroy or remove them in an instant. God is bigger, God is stronger than any silly, weak security police system. Even when they act so aggressive and intimidating, remember that according to God, they are nothing and have no power.

I like to picture David standing next to Goliath—who towers over him. Behind Goliath is this massive round shape that makes Goliath look tiny—it is God's big toe! God can crush evil powers without effort, and the fact that evil has any power at all is only because "the God of peace" has allowed it—for a time—but "will soon crush Satan under [our] feet" (Romans 16:20 ESV).

3) BAD THINGS HAPPEN TO GOOD PEOPLE SO GOD WILL BE GLORIFIED.

In John 9:3 (ESV), Jesus passes a man who was blind from birth. He is asked whose fault it was. Jesus answers: "It was not that this man sinned, or his parents, but that the works of God might be displayed in him." Your father has done nothing wrong. In fact, he has done what he is supposed to do: Tell everyone everywhere about Jesus! You should be very proud that your father was arrested. It is a sign of his obedience to Jesus' command that we preach Him and glorify Him among all peoples. God is going to use this difficult circumstance for His own glory.

We don't know how long prison will last. We don't even know how this will end for us—but that really doesn't matter. What matters is that God gets the glory in how your father acts and reacts, and in what Jesus does. When you pray for your dad, pray that he continues to act, speak, and react in such a way that the works of God are displayed in him.

4) OUR GOD IS A GOD OF DELIVERANCE.

In Daniel 3:17, three young Hebrew men are to be thrown into the fiery furnace. They tell the king: "Our God *will* deliver us." They know that God is *always* able to deliver. This is true for you. Our God can get your dad out of prison. This is an easy thing for Jesus. I am asking, trusting, and believing with you that God will do this soon.

"But," the three young Hebrew men go on, "even if he does not deliver us, we still will not bow to idols." God delivers His children usually in one of three ways:

- **Escape:** He gets us out of difficult situations, like the apostles in Acts 5:19 and Peter in Acts 12:10 being miraculously rescued from prison.

- **Endurance:** God helps us to persevere through difficult periods of prison and suffering, like Joseph in prison for many years, Jeremiah in the bottom of the well, and Paul spending several years in prison in Rome.

- **Eternity:** God takes us home to heaven where we are forever delivered from *all* evil—harm, pain, sadness, sickness, and loss. We don't always get to choose how God delivers us (and of course it is natural to want escape) but we do have this confidence: *God always delivers!* God always wins in the end! Our God *will* deliver us.

5) THE SUFFERING YOUR FAMILY IS EXPERIENCING IS NORMAL.

What you as a family are experiencing (your dad, your mom, you as children) is the normal Christian life for all who radically follow Jesus. You are not special (either in the bad way, being picked on, or in the good way, being better than anyone else). The Bible says in Philippians 1:29 (NKJV), "To you it has been granted on behalf of Christ, not only to believe in Him, but also to suffer for His sake." And in 2 Timothy 3:12 (NKJV), "All who desire to live godly in Christ Jesus will suffer persecution."

All through history, across every nation, men and women, moms and dads, boys and girls have suffered and are suffering for Jesus. You are not alone, and some have it much worse than you, much worse than your father. In the Holy Spirit, you are connected in an intimate way to a vast army of Jesus followers who have been given the privilege of suffering for Jesus. Welcome to the family—the family that loves Jesus so much it is an honor to suffer for His sake!

When the apostles were imprisoned and beaten, they rejoiced "that they were counted worthy to suffer" (Acts 5:41 NKJV), and they responded by continuing publicly and privately to teach and preach that Jesus is the Christ (Acts 5:42). Suffering made them bolder. They did not cease proclaiming Jesus everywhere. Jesus evidently looks at your family, loves you deeply, trusts you fully, so much, that He says, "Look at them! They are worthy to suffer for my name. I trust them to continue to teach and preach about me!" Oh, how much the heavenly Father loves and trusts you!

6) IT IS THE DEVIL YOU SHOULD BE ANGRY AT, NOT THE PEOPLE WHO PUT YOUR DAD IN PRISON.

In Luke 23:34 (NKJV), when Jesus is being crucified, he says, "Father, forgive them, for they do not know what they do." Really, the people who put your dad in prison (and the people group and country they represent) are not angry with him; they are angry with Jesus—even if they don't know it. All false religions deny that Jesus is God, and the devil (often without the people realizing it) stirs them up to attack anyone who believes that Jesus is God and superexalts Him as the only way of salvation.

When people do hurtful things to us, it is important to recognize that the source of their anger is fear—the fear of the devil, because he knows Jesus is winning and he hates Jesus. When we understand this, it helps us to direct our anger at the devil and not at the precious people we live among. Always remember the people you live among are precious to Jesus. They are victims of the devil's lies. We forgive them because they don't really know what they are doing. They don't realize they are actually fighting against the spirit of Jesus in us; this is a fight they cannot win. We love them because even though pain comes through their hands, we realize that the source of their evil actions is the devil.

7) YOUR FATHER WANTS YOU TO GO ON LIVING AND IN FACT TO HAVE JOY!

In John 19:26-27, when Jesus was in great trouble on the cross, He was most concerned about His friends and family. Your father (whether he is taken from you for a short time or long) wants you to live well and to love life. Sometimes we feel guilty about laughing or doing normal life and fun things when our father is in prison. We can feel guilty about laughing, visiting friends, playing football, and moving on in life in a normal way—when inside we know our father is gone and life is not normal.

Your father wants you to live free, and he would be most pleased if you continue to embrace life and find joy despite your sorrow. There are times to cry and miss him and grieve, but joy and sorrow are not opposites. They can go together. You can carry the sorrow of missing your father *and* the joy of living and laughing in life—and this is not hypocritical. Laughter and tears are brothers. They are intended to live together. Perfect, sinless, eternal Jesus both laughed and cried.

When we laugh, when we continue the normal activities of life despite living in abnormal conditions, when we laugh along with our sorrow, we are sending two messages:

We are telling God that as much as we love our earthly father, we love our heavenly Father even more and we trust Him. This delights Him. When we praise Jesus despite our troubles, when it costs us to praise Him and trust Him (when we bring sacrifices with shouts of joy, as in Psalm 27:6), we please our heavenly Father incredibly.

We also communicate to the devil that he is a loser, that he *never* can win. Jesus will win, the devil will lose, and we are celebrating the end result even while we are in the middle of the struggle with much pain. You will most honor your heavenly and earthly fathers by living well and laughing with joy—along with your sorrow.

8) LIVE AND LOVE AND LAUGH.

Jesus loves you so much, and your father loves you so much. In his prison, he is not thinking about his ministry or even his friends or the people he has brought to Jesus. Do you know whom your dad spends most of his time thinking about? *You!* Your father is praying for you, and remembering all the good times you had together, and laughing at all the funny things you did when you were small, and wondering how you are doing in school, and hoping you remembered to brush your teeth this morning. He misses his wife and his children more than anything.

Your father wants you to know again that you are more important to him than any other human or any work that he has done. He loves you, loves you, loves you. You are his pride and joy. He may not be able to see you or hug you or even speak with you, but his spirit sends a constant message. Your father says, "I love you, I love you, I love you. You are my beloved child. In you I am *well* pleased."

These are challenging days (faith never denies facts), but you *will* make it. You will make it because God is good and He loves you, because your father and mother love you, because your uncles and aunts and friends around the world love you and are praying for you.

Your father wants you to *live* and *love* and *laugh.* You will best please him by mixing your joy into your sorrow, carrying them both and trusting Jesus to help you. Keep doing the normal things of life (knowing this is what your father would want, doing them even for him), and in the quiet times when you most miss him and feel his absence, it is okay to cry. Perhaps in those times, write him a letter in your journal, tell him the things you cannot tell anyone else. Tell him the simple things; tell him the serious things. Pray for him (and your mom), and then rest in the knowledge that your father loves you very, very much and that he loves Jesus so much that this suffering of separation (that you all share) is worth it because Jesus is worth it.

We are so very proud of you. We love you so very much.

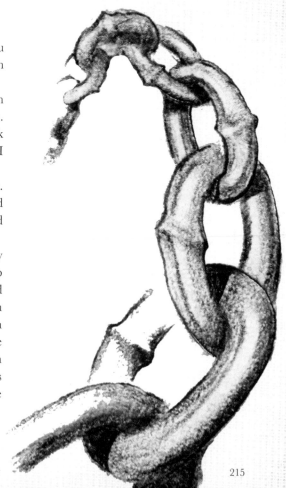

FAITH JOURNEY

STOP SIXTEEN

The Value of Character

EXTRAVAGANT DAILY TIME WITH JESUS

BY JON HODGES

I try to spend a regular time each morning and each evening in uninterrupted fellowship with Jesus. I will be the first to tell you that I do not always keep that uninterrupted time perfectly, yet it is one of the basic needs in my life and thus a priority that I strive for daily. When I am walking with Jesus daily, I am able to weather difficult storms that come my way, I am able to see God sovereign over my circumstances, and the core of my character and passions of my heart feel centered. Continual fellowship with Jesus renews my spirit and revives my soul.

My uninterrupted time with the Lord, my "quiet time," usually consists of some worship on the guitar, some Scripture reading, some listening, and some walking around the living room and speaking my heart to the Lord. It is rarely exactly the same; however, study of the Word and listening to the Lord speak are both core components of my quiet times.

MEDITATING ON THE WORD

Joshua 1:8 (NLT) counsels us: "Study this Book of Instruction continually. Meditate on it day and night so you will be sure to obey everything written in it. Only then will you prosper and succeed in all you do."

How do you study the Word? What does it mean to meditate on it versus to just read it? Do you have a plan to help you meditate on the Bible daily and nightly? Write a simple plan of Bible meditation for the week. Make note of which chapters you will read, how you will meditate on what you read, and how you might continue this meditation after this week.

LISTENING TO THE LORD

Jesus instructs us: "When you pray, don't babble on and on as people of other religions do. They think their prayers are answered merely by repeating their words again and again. Don't be like them, for your Father knows exactly what you need even before you ask him!" (Matthew 6:7-8 NLT).

How much do you listen and how much do you speak during your quiet times? Do you need to do more listening to the Lord or more speaking with the Lord? Do you ever journal what the Lord is speaking to you?

List some ways that you can actively listen to the Lord this week. How will you listen to the Lord? What will you do when He speaks to you? Will you write it down, will you record it, will you draw a picture representing it? How will you try to listen to the Lord throughout the day, not just during your quiet times?

JON HODGES

My wife, Sara, and I have had the wonderful privilege of living and working in a number of countries in the Middle East and North Africa. The Lord first burdened us in high school with a passion to see the truth of Jesus manifest among the unreached of the world. Before Sara and I even met, the Lord was preparing us and stirring us for this amazing adventure. We were married shortly after we graduated from college and left three weeks later for a pioneer field on the Arabian Peninsula where no workers from our organization had ever been.

In our first month of marriage, we arrived in our new city in the middle of the sweltering Arabian summer. The few other expatriates living in the city had left a month earlier to escape the heat, so our marriage began in a quiet Bedouin town with Arabic-speaking locals, blowing dust, and 120-degree heat as our only neighbors. Throughout the following years, we have had the opportunity to pioneer multiple projects in a number of cities throughout the Arabian Peninsula. Each new place, new opportunity, new conflict, and new challenge has given our Lord the chance to sculpt and refine our character more and more.

SUFFERING, THE GATEWAY TO CHARACTER

BY JON HODGES

Our most precious, unforgettable, and life-defining moments come during our times upon the anvil of our Lord. In his book *Abandonment to Divine Providence,* Jean Pierre de Caussade illuminates the relationship between a sculptor and a stone. Before the sculptor lies a shapeless piece of rock. The sculptor looks at that rock and envisions the beautiful work of art he is about to create. Reaching over to his box of steel instruments, he grasps the hammer, lifts it over the rock, and slams it across the rock face, smashing the first of many rough and jagged edges into what will be his creation. The sculptor sees each blow as a necessary refinement to his creation. The rock, however, only feels the cold, hard steel smashing into its form and destroying it. We often feel like that confused and tormented rock on the Lord's anvil. But take heart: It is our Master's grand vision to make you into a masterpiece.[73]

As we study character—and more specifically, the joy of submitting to the Master's perfect and complete plan to shape us more and more into the men and women He desires us to be—I challenge you to open your heart to the Lord. Before we begin, let us pray:

O sovereign Master of creation, our hearts are open to your plans. Refine us, sculpt us, and transform us into the image of Christ. We are yours, from you and for you, and we open our lives to your perfect and skillful sculpting hand. Amen.

THE GATEWAY TO CHARACTER

Not only so, but we also rejoice in our sufferings, because we know that suffering produces perseverance; perseverance, character; and character, hope. And hope does not disappoint us, because God has poured out his love into our hearts by the Holy Spirit, whom he has given us. —ROMANS 5:3-5 (NIV 84)

An old proverb says, "It's not about the destination; it's about the journey." This is certainly true regarding development of godly character. Our purpose is not to focus on our goal but to submit ourselves fully to the journey of refinement that the Lord sets us on. When we give ourselves over to the Lord's journey, without even realizing it, we will arrive at our destination and receive our reward.

The apostle Paul, in Romans 5:3, clearly charts our path. We see the first step of the journey is one of the scariest words in our dictionary, a word with so many dark and troubling connotations: *suffering*. One of the key components to our journey toward character is suffering.

OUR ATTITUDE TOWARD SUFFERING

Paul instructs us in our attitude toward suffering: Rejoice in it! What a paradox, to rejoice in something that is by definition uncomfortable, frustrating, discouraging, and painful. One of the first things we need to do on our journey to godly character is to look at suffering as an opportunity, the gateway to the destination we are striving for.

But knowing that we should rejoice when suffering comes our way doesn't mean it will be enjoyable. We—and even the great heroes of the faith—rarely feel happy about suffering. However, the Bible doesn't teach us to be happy about it, but rather to rejoice in it.

ENTER THE MAN: JOB

One of the most amazing stories of suffering, perseverance, character, and hope is that of Job, a man of great blessing and highest character. Job had integrity, devotion to the Lord, commitment to his family, and uprightness like no man on the earth.

We don't know what trials Job faced before Satan challenged God concerning him, but we can see clearly how he responded to cataclysmic suffering.

Upon hearing the horrendous news of what had befallen him—the loss of his entire family and all of his considerable possessions—Job uttered one of the most famous lines in the Bible: "The LORD gives, the LORD takes away, blessed be the name of the LORD!"

I don't think Job is standing up and doing the Ancient Near Eastern jig as he says this. I can see a man—broken, pierced, and emptied of all that he is—turning up to His God with the last few ounces of strength that he has, agonizingly squeezing out, "blessed be the name of the LORD!"

Suffering is the necessary first step toward transformation of the DNA of our souls. The opportunity to suffer helps us quickly remember what is real and what is temporary. The shaking of the temporal for a refocus on the eternal is the gift suffering brings, if we are willing to receive it. Caussade writes, "Thus, finding only deception and emptiness in everything, the soul is compelled to have recourse to God himself, and to be content with him. Happy is the soul that understands this lovingly severe conduct of God, and that corresponds faithfully with it. It is raised above all that passes away to repose in the immutable and the infinite."

So here is the first concrete challenge on our journey toward character: Rejoice in suffering. It is an opportunity, a gateway, a trumpet blow to begin the journey. Are you ready to begin? If so, then keep reading, and let the sculptor have His way.

MEDITATIONS

Clear your mind of distractions and reflect upon your attitude toward suffering. Do you find you rejoice in suffering and know it can be a part of God's plan for you?

_____

_____

_____

_____

_____

_____

We expect our weaknesses to be exposed in the process of working together in difficult contexts and embrace this exposure knowing it will lead to growth, deliverance, and wholeness.

— JON HODGES

JOURNALING

1) Write down your favorite Scripture pertaining to suffering.

_____

_____

_____

_____

_____

2) Optional: If you have a cell phone, take a photo of the Scripture you chose.

3) Make the Scripture the wallpaper on your cell phone for at least two weeks.

4) During these two weeks, recite the Scripture each time you feel like you are struggling with understanding the suffering that is occurring in your day.

PERSEVERANCE, OUR RESPONSE TO SUFFERING

BY JON HODGES

Not only so, but we also rejoice in our sufferings, because we know that suffering produces perseverance; perseverance, character; and character, hope. And hope does not disappoint us, because God has poured out his love into our hearts by the Holy Spirit, whom he has given us. —ROMANS 5:3-5 (NIV 84)

The second and most crucial step in our journey toward character is perseverance. The trials, suffering, persecution—whatever you call them—will come. There is no question. Whether you are born to a privileged Christian family in the United States or in an impoverished Muslim town in Africa, though it may look different and be of varying severity, difficulty will confront you. The question then remains: What effect will those trials have on your character? Will they fortify the DNA of your soul? Will they ground you more deeply in honesty, integrity, and humility—or will they leave you bitter, calloused, and angry? Much of this depends on whether you persevere.

225

OUR RESPONSE DETERMINES OUR GROWTH

Our response to and attitude in life's difficulties can reconstruct the DNA of our souls for the better or for the worse. Trials themselves are neutral, neither inherently good nor bad. But as we saw earlier, we should rejoice in suffering and look at it as the gateway to building godly character.

Your trial could be as ground shaking as the death of a loved one or as seemingly trivial as a disagreement with a good friend. No matter the perceived immensity of the trail before you, your response will govern your growth. So how will you respond to your trial?

I vividly remember one of our first earth-shattering trials on the field. My wife and I had arrived in one of the most gospel-resistant countries in the world, and we were ready for all types of demonic attack. We were ready to be shot at, targeted for kidnapping, spat upon, assaulted by manifest demons that would oppose God's work. We were ready! What we weren't prepared for was a painful and unexpected disagreement with a friend, believer, and colleague. We had thought we had prepared for it all, but here we were being attacked in the very area we had the least experience in. Isn't our God good to give us just the kinds of trials we need to grow us in the areas of our greatest weakness?

Those nights were agonizing, filled with frustration, anger, and bitterness. This trial brought out all shapes and forms of a monster living inside of me that I never knew resided there. The disagreement and my reaction to it shook the foundations of so many areas of my life that I had thought were solid. The poisons of bad attitude and hate began creeping up. I was ashamed of my response. This was the beautifully painful process of the reconstruction of my spiritual DNA. After months of dealing with the issue, I hit my fork in the road. My negative responses up to that point had been a natural reaction reflecting the current state of my character, and the Lord and my friends began to challenge me to shift my attitude, to put down my flesh, and to persevere.

Little by little, I started to identify areas of my spirit and character that needed change. It was by the grace of God and through the help of the Holy Spirit that I was able to ask forgiveness where I was wrong and to intentionally begin to change my attitude. Piece by piece, the Lord was tearing out coal that had attached itself to my character and was replacing it with His jewels.

About a year into this episode, the Lord gave me an epiphany that I will never forget. As I sat in my car, having just finished a phone call with the person with whom I had had the conflict, the Lord dropped on me every area that I had been wrong in my spirit. Surprisingly, it was one of the most amazing feelings of freedom I have ever experienced. All I wanted to do was call all my close friends and tell them how the Lord had graciously broken me and corrected my arrogant and prideful attitude. A major piece of my character had been reconstructed, and I could not have felt better.

For every story of perseverance, however, there is a story of heartbreak. I can think of good friends here on the field who went through heavy trials and left bitter at the world, angry at God, and making decisions that represented broken character. Our hearts go out to them. I know I have failed at times as well. But even our failures to persevere are opportunities to grow if we open our hearts to humility and the work of the Holy Spirit. The important thing is that we strive with all we have to allow the Lord to refine us. And when we fall, we get up, brush off the dust, bandage the wounds, and keep going forward. Perseverance is not an easy process, but it is essential if we want to grow in our character.

WAITING IN THE LORD'S PRESENCE

As King David did, ask God to search you, know you, find if there is any evil way in you, and to lead you in the path everlasting. As you spend time waiting in the Lord's presence, ask Him to both convict you and commend you. As much as we should look for the Lord's conviction, we should meditate on His commendation. Make note of what the Lord is telling you, and begin asking Him daily to sharpen you in those areas.

THE REWARD OF OUR JOURNEY

BY JON HODGES

Not only so, but we also rejoice in our sufferings, because we know that suffering produces perseverance; perseverance, character; and character, hope. And hope does not disappoint us, because God has poured out his love into our hearts by the Holy Spirit, whom he has given us. —ROMANS 5:3-5 (NIV 84)

Six months after starting karate classes, the day of my test for my gold belt arrived. It was my sophomore year of high school, and I had been training hard week after week to develop my body and skills. I'd thought about quitting a few times along the way but decided to keep pushing myself.

On the day of the test, my instructor started me off with a warm-up of sit-ups, push-ups, stretches, and the splits. I then demonstrated all of the katas that I was to have learned to that point. Then the sparring came—oh, did it come. Already exhausted from the warm-ups and katas, they put me in round after round of sparring matches, each time with more-experienced, higher-belted students. I felt it would never end. My partner would spar until he was tired, then a fresh student was sent in.

When I could take no more sparring, my instructor capped off my test with a circle spar. All of the other students circled around me and one by one threw moves at me that I had to deflect. After my instructor noticed I was taking more hits than deflecting, he had mercy on me and ended the test.

I stood for my review while my instructor conferred with others. After a few minutes, he walked toward me stern-faced. "You passed this test with flying colors," he said. "We would like to award you an extra stripe on your belt, and invite you to be a part of our competition team."

Six months earlier, I could barely do thirty push-ups, but now I was on top of the world! I had a gold belt, a green stripe, and purple pants signifying I was part of the competition team. I was a new man! I could take on anything! The tests and trials had changed me.

I love the reward that comes after a difficult endeavor, but the trophy or ribbon or purple pants are only symbols of the accomplishment that has taken place inside the recipient. The trophy is a reminder that you are not the same. This is also true in our journey toward character.

A trophy waits at the end of this journey through suffering and perseverance: the building of our character. You will obtain the reward of looking a bit more like that amazing sculpture the Master is making you into. If you have opened your heart to the Lord's refinement during your trial, you will come out changed. You will not only act more honestly, you will be more honest. People won't just perceive you as having integrity; you will be a man or woman of integrity. The more the Lord allows you to suffer under His powerful and precise hammer of refinement, the more you become a person of character.

SEVEN JEWELS OF GODLY CHARACTER

There are many important elements that would be integrated into the soul of a person of character. Proverbs 6 includes seven character flaws the Lord hates. By examining them, we can identify their opposites, seven jewels of godly character that He delights in, and ask Him to begin transforming us in these areas.

Proverbs 6:16-19 (NIV 84) reads: "There are six things the LORD hates, seven that are detestable to him: haughty eyes, a lying tongue, hands that shed innocent blood, a heart that devises wicked schemes, feet that are quick to rush into evil, a false witness who pours out lies, and a man who stirs up dissension among brothers."

Jewel 1, Humility: God, grant me humility; destroy my haughty eyes.

One of the pitfalls we can face while working on a team is pride. The temptations to presume that I know it better than others, I'm more capable, or I should be the team leader are common flaws of character that run through the minds of individuals on ministry teams. The temptation to compare our abilities to others is rooted in pride.

Let us pray that the Lord would instill humility in every area of our being.

Jewel 2, Honesty: God, instill honesty in my life; destroy my lying tongue.

Do we model honesty? Are we transparent enough to let others know our weaknesses? Do we speak truth to our friends, family, and leadership?

Let's pray that the Lord grants us favor and wisdom in this area.

Jewel 3, Compassion: God, make me passionate to heal; destroy my tendency to shed innocent blood.

Are we healers? Do we seek wholeness for ourselves and others? Do our words uplift, encourage, and exhort—or do they degrade, humiliate, and cut down?

Many of us struggle with this character defect, shedding innocent blood, without even realizing it. We love to joke with friends and pick on them about different things. When someone does something we consider stupid, we love to make sure everyone remembers it. It is good and even healthy for joking together; however, our jokes can quickly turn to cutting and unfair jabs that can destroy trust and unity. (See Ephesians 5:4.)

Let's pray that the Lord grants us the privilege to be people of compassion.

Jewel 4, Self-control: God, make me a person of self-control; keep me from planning wicked schemes.

The battlefield of the mind is strategic in our spiritual lives. The mind is where we wish good upon others or wish them harm. The mind creates good plans to love God and stay away from sin, while at the same time planning different ways to be deceitful or give in to sinful desires.

A person of self-control will plan ways to fight temptation before it even comes. A self-controlled person holds his or her tongue rather than snapping a quick response.

Let's pray we control our sinful desires by proactively planning for good.

Jewel 5, Contentment: God, make me a person of contentment; keep me from rushing toward evil things.

We often seek out sinful acts because there is something in us that is not content in Christ. Many times, we rush to evil because we lack contentment. Not being content with our possessions, we steal; not content in our marriages, we lust; not content losing an argument, we react in anger.

Let us pray as Jesus taught His disciples to pray, "Lord, keep me from temptation and deliver me from the evil one." Evil is just an arm's reach away. Often we don't even need to physically act out to give in to temptation. As we follow Jesus, and especially as we engage in the front lines of the spiritual battle, the enemy will tempt us in our weakest areas.

Satan has little internal ammunition to use against those who are content in Jesus, content in their marriage, and content in their possessions.

Let us pray the Lord begins to transform us now. Where do you need transformation?

Jewel 6, Truth: God, make me a person passionate for the truth; keep me from being a false witness.

Let us examine how we talk about others. Do we say things about others that are fair and honest? Do we seek truth at the core of our relationships?

Let us pray that the Lord will make us people of truth.

Jewel 7, Unity: God, make me a person who promotes unity; keep me from stirring up dissension among believers.

A person of unity is one who constantly gives preference to others. This is a person of Philippians 2 who does nothing out of selfish ambition or vain conceit, but in humility values others above him- or herself, looking to the interests of others.

Are we ready to submit to others, even when we don't love what we are submitting to? Are we ready to patiently prefer others' opinions to ours for the sake of unity? This is one of the most difficult character jewels to live out, but one of the most beneficial to the body of Christ.

Let's pray the Lord kills our pride and makes us people who, as servants of Christ, walk in unity with others.

MEDITATIONS

The missionary writes about "The Seven Jewels of Godly Character." Review these seven points, and choose the top three you feel God wants you to hone.

_____

_____

_____

_____

_____

_____

_____

_____

_____

_____

Who we are will drive what we do. Integrity, humility, and authenticity are just as important as competence.

— JON HODGES

JOURNALING

1) Select three pens or markers of different colors.

2) For each of the three "jewels" you chose from the meditation on the previous page, write one word relating to it. For example, if you chose "honesty," write a word next to it that makes you think of being honest.

3) Now draw any kind of line that connects all of the words.

Optional:

1) Use several other colored pens or markers to draw a crown with seven jewels.

2) Within the jewels on the crown, write the names of the "seven jewels of godly character."

3) Free your creative side to embellish the crown and pray that the jewels of God would be sprinkled throughout the Muslim world.

Life & Death

One thing in life is inevitable.
Death.
Jesus gave us confidence in death.
Life beyond it.
Joy in it.
Triumph over it.

No fear in death.
No guilt in life.
This is our freedom.

GALATIANS 5

ARTIST: MICHAEL BUESKING | WORK: "PICTURES AT AN EXECUTION"

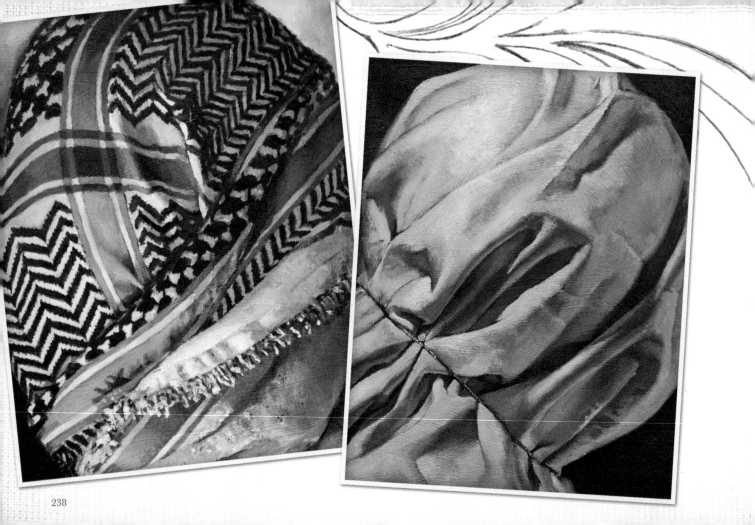

PERSPECTIVE

When you look at these paintings, what do you see? Do you see death or life transitioning beyond earth? When you look at these paintings, what do you feel? Do you feel fear or peace beyond understanding?

Surprisingly, few missionaries to the Arab world suffer death. Yet, news coverage paints a different picture for you. Are you willing to face your fear of death if God calls you?

AND HE SAID TO ALL,

If anyone would come after me, let him deny himself and take up his cross daily and follow me.

LUKE 9:23 (ESV)

And so began
my real-life
ministry schooling.
I thought I would learn
HOW TO MINISTER
TO OTHERS;
little did I realize
how much ministry
I personally needed.

— ABRAHAM DAVIS

STOP SEVENTEEN

The Value of Lifelong Learning

ABRAHAM & SARAH DAVIS

When we met, we were both preparing to serve in global ministry among the unreached. While our hearts ached for the lost, the prospect of serving in the Middle East was not appealing. Eventually, the Lord reconciled our hearts to the desperate need and the calling He had placed on our lives. In the three short years since we first arrived in the Middle East, we have grown to love our Arab neighbors and friends. Our daily prayer is that God will continue to broaden our hearts and minds, and that He will give us a greater capacity for service in this land.

EXTRAVAGANT DAILY TIME WITH JESUS

BY ABRAHAM & SARAH DAVIS

Our daily abiding time includes these practices:

PRAYER

We both tend to be introspective meditators as we process what is happening in our lives. While we verbally acknowledge our thoughts and needs, most of our prayers are quiet conversations with our Father. We thank Him profusely for His goodness, grace, and gifts in our lives, and His abundant love and redemption. Every morning and evening, we read the Scripture and pray together with our two young sons. Then, on a weekly basis, we meet with prayer partners.

We are provoked to intercede and seek for miraculous breakthroughs as we encounter needs in our own lives and in the lives of those around us. We ask the Lord to respond in power and in a decisive fashion, which will resolve the issues and allow others to see His glory as a result.

BIBLE READING

This is an area where systematizing and spontaneity work in tandem. Most of the time, we individually work through a book in the Bible chapter by chapter, and as topics arise through conversations, sermon reflections, etc., we will meander from day to day in our reading. We like to read a study Bible and frequently bounce to verses annotated in the margins.

MEMORIZATION

Most of the memorization we have done in recent years has been trying to capture key verses in Arabic fluently enough to be able to share them in conversations with the contacts the Lord gives us.

We are provoked to intercede and seek for miraculous breakthroughs as we encounter needs in our own lives and in the lives of those around us. — ABRAHAM & SARAH DAVIS

A COMMITMENT TO LIFELONG LEARNING

BY ABRAHAM DAVIS

"Ask, and it will be given to you; seek, and you will find; knock, and it will be opened to you. For everyone who asks receives, and the one who seeks finds, and to the one who knocks it will be opened." —MATTHEW 7:7-8 (ESV)

In the late 1990s, while we were still in college, God placed in our hearts the desire to serve in the Muslim Middle East. In preparation, we sought to learn as much as we could and gain practical ministerial experience. Because I had completed a ministry internship with an ethnic fellowship in a Midwestern city, I thought I had a decent grip on pastoral ministry, and after working nearly two years in corporate America, I felt ready to pursue a full-time pastoral position as the next step in preparing for full-time overseas gospel work.

Through a series of providential encounters, we had an interview at a nontraditional church on the outskirts of the city with a nontraditional pastor known as the "Biker Pastor." He was known for his penchant for riding Harley-Davidson motorcycles and racing in motocross competitions, not to mention his numerous tattoos and skull jewelry. Needless to say, he didn't fit my mental profile of a potential personal mentor. Yet God proved, once again, that He knows what is best for me (1 Corinthians 1:25-29).

After our first meeting and interview, Biker Pastor made a statement I will never forget. It went something like this: "Now that you've finished Bible college, your real education can begin. I am going to help you unlearn everything you learned."

My initial thought was, *Who does he think he is? That is arrogant! I spent lots of money, time, tears, hours, and effort to apply myself in the learning of how to do "God's work."* That was one of my many problems. I had studied what I should do and how I should do it, but I hadn't really done it. This man had. He and his father had pioneered a church with eighteen people meeting in a basement. After being a mobile congregation for nearly eight years, they had acquired their first building. By the time I came along in their growth process, they were in their second building program, had more than ten full-time staff members, and they were mothering another church to health and autonomy. Their years of sacrifice made it possible for me to come and be a full-time pastor at a stable ministry center with ample resources and personnel. Who did I think I was? I was the arrogant one.

And so began my real-life ministry schooling. I thought I would learn how to minister to others; little did I realize how much ministry I personally needed. I soon became painfully aware that I wasn't truly living Jesus' promises about asking, seeking, and knocking in Matthew 7:7-10 (ESV). You see, those promises of receiving, finding, and having the door opened to you are sandwiched between two conditional statements in verses 1-6 and verse 12:

"Judge not, that you be not judged. For with the judgment you pronounce you will be judged, and with the measure you use it will be measured to you. Why do you see the speck that is in your brother's eye, but do not notice the log that is in your own eye? Or how can you say to your brother, 'Let me take the speck out of your eye,' when there is the log in your own eye? You hypocrite, first take the log out of your own eye, and then you will see clearly to take the speck out of your brother's eye [vv. 1-6]. . . . So whatever you wish that others would do to you, do also to them, for this is the Law and the Prophets [v. 12]."

I liked the idea of seeing people come to Christ and follow in His ways, just as I had done as a seventeen-year-old. Yet I had forgotten, or at the very least not appreciated, from where the Lord had brought me. I found ministering to dysfunctional and stubborn people a bit irritating, and at times found myself wondering, *Why don't they stop doing this?* or *Why can't they see this is the problem?* My thoughts filled with a host of other criticisms. Thankfully, Pastor Biker gently showed me my own lack of grace

and compassion for people. He taught me that ministry isn't patting people on the back when they finally leave their filthy, sinful ways; rather it is loving people while they are still wallowing in the mud of rebellion, foolishness, and godlessness. That's doing to others as I wish they would do to me.

The truth was that I had a huge plank in my eye that was keeping me from being able to "clearly see how to take the speck out of [my] brother's eye." I wouldn't dare say I am a cured "plank porter," but I have come to terms with my own affinity for that well-worn wooden eye accoutrement. I must constantly ask God to show me its hideousness and remove it, so that I might receive all that He has for me. My desire is to be able to share with others a view of the Holy One with an unobstructed vision.

But first, I had to learn to appreciate how much I had been forgiven—even though I hadn't lived a profligate life of drunkenness, drug addiction, robbery, gang violence, or promiscuity. My thoughts had not always been pure, and my heart had harbored the insidious, hideous sin of judging others with a harsher standard than I used for myself. I failed to accept people and love them as the Lord loved me. I realized I needed to love the Lord more and allow His love to flow through me to His lost sheep. It also dawned on me how foolish it was to expect people who are not in a covenant relationship with God nor renewed by the Holy Spirit to live according to biblical principles. Even we who walk with the Lord and have been filled with the Holy Spirit struggle to walk as Jesus walked. How impossible it is for those who don't even know Him!

MEDITATIONS

Do you minister to others but know in your heart you are the one who needs to be ministered to?

_____

_____

Does stubborn pride or a feeling that you know it all ever hold you back from allowing someone to minister to you?

_____

_____

If you answered yes to either of the above questions, search your heart: In what areas do you need ministry? What must you change in order to receive ministry from others?

_____

_____

_____

JOURNALING

1) Think about three times in your life when you were able to learn something—about yourself or ministry, for example—from an unexpected source. Write a few sentences about the lessons you learned in those circumstances.

_____

_____

_____

_____

_____

_____

_____

_____

2) Ask God to send people into your life—like the Biker Pastor—who can mentor you and show you areas in which you need to grow.

THE KEY INGREDIENT: HUMILITY

BY ABRAHAM & SARAH DAVIS

Trust in the Lord with all your heart, and do not lean on your own understanding. In all your ways acknowledge him, and he will make straight your paths. Be not wise in your own eyes . . . —PROVERBS 3:5-7A (ESV)

Coming to the Arab world to learn Arabic was a humbling experience. We both were bilingual before arriving in the Middle East, and we had both experienced a modicum of "success" in our previous careers and ministries in the States. We knew we would face many challenges, so we arrived in the Middle East with what we considered to be measured expectation.

Still, it became apparent within the first three months that we were in for far more than we had bargained for. It was in this crucible that we had to make learning from God the principal priority in our lives. A partial undertaking wouldn't cut it. It had to be the pursuit that eclipsed all others. "Trust in the Lord with *all* your heart" underscores that we must grant God the preeminent place of governing all of our faculties. Our "heart" includes our mind/intellect, our emotions, and our will/volition. God wants us to love Him with all of our being.

Although Proverbs 3:6-7 warns us not to "lean on [our] own understanding" and "be not wise in [our] own eyes," sadly and painfully, it took us quite a while to grasp this fact. We soon felt overwhelmed by all that had transpired in our first year in the Middle East. We couldn't depend on our own understanding and wisdom. They were inadequate. But the same passage in Proverbs gave us direction. It told us to acknowledge the Lord in all of our ways. The verb *acknowledge* here literally means "to know" God in every domain of life.

Obviously, God's revelation (His Word) is the clearest avenue for knowing God; yet, God also repeatedly instructs us to consult other godly individuals in our quest to know and follow Him. The Wisdom writers state, "Without counsel plans fail, but with many advisers they succeed" (Proverbs 15:22 ESV). "The way of a fool is right in his own eyes, but a wise man listens to advice" (Proverbs 12:15 ESV). "Better was a poor and wise youth than an old and foolish king who no longer knew how to take advice" (Ecclesiastes 4:13 ESV). Indeed, while God's instructions are pure guidance, our crooked and perverse hearts can easily lead us astray without the balancing influence of mature, stable, and proven servants of God to lend insight.

Looking back over our lives and ministry, we have been blessed as numbers of wise people have stepped in and offered crucial counsel at various crossroads. Perhaps the most important has been the godly advice we have consistently received from Sarah's father and mother. Becoming a lifelong learner requires that one continually orients his or her heart to receive and respond to the input of other godly people that God places in our lives.

Let's look for a moment at the life of Moses. Here's a man with whom God talked as a friend—face to face (Exodus 33:11). He was commissioned for service out of the burning bush on Mt. Horeb (Exodus 3). He received the Ten Commandments from God's hand on Mt. Sinai (Exodus 31:18; Deuteronomy 9:10). He summited the mountain of God and stayed in His presence forty days and nights (Exodus 24). God revealed both His glory and His personal name to Moses (Exodus 34). His epitaph reveals that no other prophet arose in Israel like Moses who knew God so intimately. No other did such miracles and awesome deeds in the sight of all Israel (Deuteronomy 34:10-12) until Jesus came. Yet, in the midst of these sublime moments of revelation and intimacy with God, Exodus 18 reveals that Moses was overwhelmed by his responsibilities and duties. He was frazzled and fatigued, and God sent a counselor with the words of wisdom that he needed to achieve balance in his life.

In Exodus 18:13-24 (ESV), we see Moses working from morning until evening, resolving disputes the people have brought before him. His father-in-law, Jethro, confronts him: "What you are doing is not good. You and the people with you will certainly wear yourselves out, for the thing is too heavy for you. You are not able to do it alone." Jethro advises Moses to appoint "able men from all the people" to serve as "chiefs of thousands, of hundreds, of fifties, and of tens." These men would handle minor disputes, leaving Moses only to decide on great matters. "So Moses listened to the voice of his father-in-law and did all that he had said."

This is a stunning account! Jethro sees the excessive demands placed on his son-in-law, and he intervenes with a command: "Obey my voice; I will give you advice, and God be with you!" What audacity! Yes, Jethro was a "priest of Midian," but he should be the one receiving advice from Moses—not giving it to him. However, Moses listens to the words of his aged father-in-law and does exactly what he advises. As a result, Moses' load is lightened and elder leadership is developed in Israel. Had he not listened to Jethro's timely advice, perhaps Moses would have "burned out," and potential leaders may not have risen to the occasion.

Now, let's contrast Moses' response to his learning opportunity with that of King Rehoboam's (1 Kings 12). Rehoboam inherited the throne upon the death of his wise but wayward father, King Solomon. The people were tired of providing conscripted labor for the kingdom, and they asked Rehoboam for relief. Initially, he called the elders together and asked their advice. They counseled him to comply with the people's request, but Rehoboam wasn't satisfied. He then asked the young men who had grown up with him for their counsel. They encouraged him to increase the pressure on the people. Undoubtedly, this jibed with Rehoboam's own ambitious and egotistical bent, and rather than humbling himself according to the wise counsel of the elders, he answered the people harshly. The result was that the ten northern tribes rebelled and seceded from the kingdom. Only the tribe of Judah accepted Rehoboam as their king. Jeroboam became king of the ten northern tribes and guided them into religious apostasy and compromise that eventually led to their captivity and loss of identity as Israelites.

Scripture repeatedly teaches we gain more than we gamble when we listen to godly counsel and learn from the experience and insight of others. Consider carefully and prayerfully before labeling godly counsel as obsolete, not with the times, or naïve. Remember, "Whoever walks with the wise becomes wise, but the companion of fools will suffer harm" (Proverbs 13:20 ESV).

THE KNOWLEDGE OF GOD

BY ABRAHAM & SARAH DAVIS

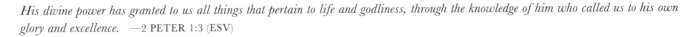

His divine power has granted to us all things that pertain to life and godliness, through the knowledge of him who called us to his own glory and excellence. —2 PETER 1:3 (ESV)

Our call as followers of Christ is to reflect His glory and excellence as we live with Him, in Him, and for Him. As we behold His glory and goodness, we project to others the splendid light that He shines on us. God has granted to us the privilege of being glory-bearers for Him in a world filled with darkness, perverseness, deception, confusion, and corruption.

Peter says that God's divine power has "granted to us *all* things that pertain to life and godliness." This means there is no deficiency in what God has given us. There is nothing more that He could or should do in order to ensure that we can possess life and live in a godly manner. That's a bold claim for one who found himself slipping into cowardice, prejudice, and error on more than one occasion.

This fisherman-turned-apostle states that we gain access to these treasures "through the knowledge of him who called us." In fact, the previous verse states, "May grace and peace be multiplied to you *in the knowledge of* God and of Jesus our Lord." Simon Peter is basically saying that grace and peace are multiplied or made abundant in our lives through our knowledge of God and Jesus

Christ. This is the linchpin or central supporting element required for living a godly life. In fact, Peter uses the concept of knowledge or knowing (the Greek word is ἐπίγνωσις /epignosis or a derivative) five times in the first ten verses of his second epistle.

Not only do we gain grace, peace, life, and godliness through our knowledge of Him who called us, but Peter challenges us to constantly increase in faith, virtue, self-control, steadfastness, brotherly affection, and love. As these qualities increase in our lives, they will keep us from being ineffective or unfruitful. Thus our effectiveness and fruitfulness are directly related to our knowledge of the Holy One! If we allow our knowledge of Him to become stagnant, we won't simply retain what we have—we will actually regress. On the other hand, if we are "diligent" and "practice these qualities," Peter states we will "never fall."

Peter's comments on the knowledge of God are surprisingly profound for a Galilean fisherman. He may have been "uneducated and common" from a worldly viewpoint, but because he "had been with Jesus" (Acts 4:13) and was filled with the Holy Spirit, his knowledge of God and his experience with the Divine equipped him and made him anything but normal. Scripture allows us to observe Peter's profound metamorphosis from one who denied Jesus during the Passion narrative (Mark 14:66-72) to his pervasive leadership in the early church.

He guided the selection process of another apostle to replace Judas (Acts 1:15-26) and preached a powerful sermon on the Day of Pentecost that resulted in 3,000 new converts (2:14-40). He healed the lame man at the temple gate and then preached to those who witnessed the miracle (3:6-26). He answered the Sanhedrin when called to account for the disturbance in the temple precinct (4:8-13). He pronounced the death penalty upon Ananias and Sapphira for their deception, and they instantly fell dead at his feet (5:1-10). He unabashedly corrected and threatened Simon the Sorcerer in Samaria (8:18-24). Yet, we find an insightful look at Peter's internal conflict and continued spiritual growth in Acts 10.

The chapter opens with God's revelation of Himself to Cornelius, a Roman centurion. Because of Cornelius's piety and devotion, God chose him to be the catalytic agent that sparked the gospel's spread among Gentliles who had not converted to Judaism. The next day, the story continues at the home of Simon the tanner in Joppa. Peter was faithfully abiding in Christ and praying on the flat roof of the tanner's home. About noon, he fell into a trance and had a vision that confused his devout Jewish sensibilities. He was told to "rise, kill and eat" all kinds of animals, reptiles, and birds that were declared ceremonially unclean in the Torah. When Peter

> I failed
> to accept
> people and
> love them
> as the Lord
> loved me.
>
> — ABRAHAM DAVIS

protested, God responded, "What God has made clean, do not call common" (Acts 10:15). Luke records that this scenario played out three times, and while Peter was still struggling to understand the meaning of the vision, Cornelius's emissaries arrived at the front door asking for Peter.

The following day, Peter accompanied Cornelius's representatives back to his home in Caesarea. As he entered, Cornelius fell at his feet in reverence, and Peter reminded him that he was just a man. Peter's initial comments to the group that had gathered reminded them that it was unlawful for a Jewish man to enter a Gentile's home because it was considered ceremonially unclean. But then he quickly added, "But God has shown me that I should not call any person common or unclean. So when I was sent for, I came without objection. I ask then why you sent for me" (Acts 10:28-29 ESV).

Whew! Can you conceive the monumental negative impact on evangelism and the spread of the gospel if Peter had not understood that God wanted him to visit a Gentile home, and that God, Himself, was calling Gentiles to follow Him? Imagine a whole slice of humanity being delayed entry into Christ's Kingdom. In the first eight chapters of Acts, we see Peter transformed from a fisherman to a preacher who exhorts thousands, performs miracles, and stands up to the same religious leaders who had crucified Jesus just a few months earlier, and calls down divine destruction on deceptive believers and sorcerers. Yet when it came to visiting a Gentile home, Peter was bound by traditions he would not and could not break. It was such a huge hurdle that God had to interrupt and confront Peter three times during prayer in order to keep him from being ineffective or unfruitful because he lacked knowledge of our Lord Jesus Christ.

When the news spread about the events at Cornelius's house, the Jewish believers were critical of Peter's actions until they heard how Cornelius's guests had also been baptized with the Holy Spirit in the same way they had received the Holy Spirit in the Upper Room. This was Peter's defense: "'If then God gave the same gift to them as he gave to us when we believed in the Lord Jesus Christ, who was I that I could stand in God's way?' When they heard these things, they fell silent. And they glorified God, saying, 'Then to the Gentiles also God has granted repentance that leads to life'" (Acts 11:17-18 ESV).

A further indicator of Peter's prestige among the early church leaders emerges in Acts 15 during the First Council at Jerusalem. In this council, the leaders discussed whether Gentile believers were required to observe Jewish law. Peter stood and said, "Why are you putting God to the test by placing a yoke on the neck of the disciples that neither our fathers nor we have been able to bear? But we believe that we will be saved through the grace of the Lord Jesus, just as they will" (Acts 15:10-11 ESV). Peter's remarks silenced the crowd, and after they listened to Paul and Barnabas recount the stories of the signs and wonders God had done through them as they worked among the Gentiles, James the Elder made the final decision. The observance of Jewish laws and traditions would not be required of Gentile converts.

As encouraging as that breakthrough was, Paul tells us that Peter continued to struggle with his anti-Gentile bias even after his experience at Cornelius's house and the First Council in Jerusalem (see Galatians 2:11-14).

The ethnic unity and cross-cultural diversity that Paul and Barnabas worked so hard to establish in the Antioch church was being undermined by Judaizers who came from Jerusalem and James the Elder. They belonged to a group of Jewish Christians who continued to believe that Old Testament customs and dietary restrictions were necessary for all believers. Although Peter understood that God accepted Gentiles without partiality, he rejected what he knew to be true out of fear of criticism from those in the Jerusalem church. Even Barnabas, Paul's coworker, succumbed to the persuasive Judaizers and "was led astray by their hypocrisy."

This incident in Antioch illustrates that even the greatest men and women of God can have blind spots, harbor bigotry and prejudices, and be vulnerable to deception. One doesn't have to look far in church history to find eminent figures who had real issues with people groups they found offensive. Regardless of the blind spots of others, the real question we must ask is, "God, what blind spot or prejudice is keeping me from obeying you fully?" Indeed, Paul's warning to the Corinthians—"Therefore let anyone who thinks that he stands take heed lest he fall" (1 Corinthians 10:12 ESV)—was just as germane for Peter and Barnabas as it is for us today.

People are people,
no matter where you are in the world.
I think about the ladies I've met here—
each with *personalities,*
dreams, and hobbies
that remind me of
family and friends
back home.

— A MISSIONARY
IN JEDDAH

FAITH JOURNEY

STOP EIGHTEEN

A Walk Through Jeddah

A WALK THROUGH JEDDAH

JEDDAH

I pick up my tall mocha at the counter and turn to leave the local Starbucks. I walk out into the fading sunlight as a couple of guys on Harley-Davidsons roll in. My husband and I walk across the parking lot and head for the walking path beside the sea. I feel the wind blow off the water. It is another hot, humid day, making me grateful again for the sea breeze.

The whole area along the waterfront has filled up tonight. There are men running and women power-walking, kids flying kites, and families picnicking. We watch the last few jet-skiers coming off the water and Filipino men fishing along the shore. We pass a little kid selling mint-flavored gum and trinkets and those glow-stick things. He's hard to resist. We give him about six riyals for some gum and a glow-in-the-dark necklace. It's on nights like these that I feel a little homesick. I mean, seeing all the people, the picnics, the glow sticks—it's like the Fourth of July here. Except it's not. This isn't Jacksonville; it's Jeddah. It's not America; it's Saudi Arabia. Life is so different here, but sometimes it feels familiar.

We continue our walk along the Corniche, the stretch of beaches and coves that runs the length of Jeddah along the Red Sea, breathing in both the smell of the sea and food cooking. We keep glancing at the horizon to make sure we don't miss the sunset. Earlier in the evening, families claimed their spots in the coves with their mats, and now they set out their picnics and coffee pots and relax, enjoying various things like rotisserie chicken, French fries, salad, seasoned rice, and orange juice. This evening we skipped the picnic and went for burgers and fries from a nearby snack stand.

While the surroundings feel like any park in America, the people are quite an assortment. I see the women, including myself, in abayas, but as the sun fades it is difficult to tell which wear the traditional black and which wear the newly fashionable blues and purples. Every woman has her head covered, though I don't notice any fully veiled faces tonight. There are as many men in traditional white thobes with red-and-white-checked scarves as there are in business suits and shorts and jeans and T-shirts. Come to think of it, even those guys back at the Starbucks riding the Harleys were wearing leather and Harley jackets.

We find a place to sit. My husband and I discovered that people are friendly but tend to keep to themselves unless we approach them. Tonight we sit down with our snacks and greet the family next to us. "Salam alaykum. Kayf halik?" ("Peace be upon you. How are you?") They seem surprised and excited to hear us speak Arabic. They simply answer, "Al-humd-i-Allah" ("Praise God"). We meet many people around town, while running errands, just by saying hello and asking questions. Americans rarely speak Arabic or show knowledge of the culture, so whenever we do, immediately people want to connect. Often, after a few minutes, we exchange phone numbers and make plans to meet for dinner, coffee, or shopping trips. From there, friendships go deep fast.

In fact, I'm really looking forward to tomorrow evening. We're having dinner with a local Muslim family that also happens to be our biggest support system in this city. I get a bit overwhelmed when I think about them. If it weren't for this family, it would have been difficult to stay here early on. They helped us work through the issues of getting settled into our new place when we arrived, showing us such kindness, hospitality, and acceptance. It is amazing how they have made us feel like family.

Muslim identity and family are everything to these people. Most of the extended family lives nearby, and they see each other regularly throughout the week at one or more family dinners. And while that seems different from my family back home, where we see each other only once or twice a year for holidays, the relationships between siblings and parents and grandparents are so much like my own. They love and care for each other. They argue and fight but always make up, and they watch out for one another. When I am with our Muslim friends, I feel like I am watching my own family.

I look around at all the people hanging out along the Corniche tonight, and I can't help but smile. Because people are people, no matter where you are in the world. I think about the ladies I've met here—each with personalities, dreams, and hobbies that remind me of family and friends back home.

Breaking into our peaceful picnic is the screech of tires along the thoroughfare. "Kids these days," my husband says. And he's right, though maybe he shouldn't be laughing. Somewhere down the street now is a car of young guys pulling stunts. All that screeching of tires is a favorite pastime, a.k.a. drifting, or the art of acceleration before slamming on the brakes. It can be fascinating to watch but pretty dangerous and frowned upon by the government. But that doesn't always stop the bored, the daring, and the young from trying whatever crazy thing comes to their head.

This country is very young. The median age is around twenty-six. Think of it: Half the population is under twenty-six years old. With such a young population comes modernization. These young people remind me of young Americans. They are into mobile phones, Facebook, Twitter, YouTube, video games, you name it. They are engaged in the world around them, and they are a diverse group, difficult to generalize—some are fanatical, others more open-minded, with various levels of education and connection to urban culture.

Starbucks, Harleys, families picnicking, the youth, they all make Jeddah look very much like the West at times, but it's also a place where I never feel fully settled. I think my husband and I realize we don't have forever; each day is a little bit like borrowed time. Any day we could be kindly asked to leave. That reality can make pleasant nights like this on the Corniche very sobering. I sip my mocha, we eat our burgers, and looking around I see a lot of people who don't know Christ. I think of our Muslim friends, our family here, and other faces that we don't yet know, and I pray that God gives us connections tonight, tomorrow, tomorrow night, for as long as He will, and that we won't pass up any opportunity to say "Salam alaykum."

The Role of the Holy Spirit in Maintaining a Soft Heart in Hard Times

THE ROLE OF THE HOLY SPIRIT IN MAINTAINING A SOFT HEART IN HARD TIMES

BY MARK RENFROE

Kris and Jaime and their kids have been serving on a Live Dead Arab World church-planting team for the past few years. They have great relationships with the people among whom they serve. The road hasn't been easy, but they were just starting to see fruit when they were forced by the host government to leave the country. They are hurting emotionally and confused about their future.

Dear Kris and Jaime,

I know you are hurting. Amy and I have been where you are now. It was only a few years ago when we were forced out of our adopted homeland. The Lord had helped us make this country our home. Our kids had learned the language fluently. When they spoke of "home," they weren't speaking of somewhere on the other side of the world. Our friends were there. I can still remember the heartbreak I felt that night while being held in the airport police station and being told that I would not be allowed to return to my home. Amy and the kids were twenty-five miles away, but it might as well have been 2,500 miles. In that moment, I also felt like God was thousands of miles away. Over the next few weeks, the Lord taught me several important lessons. Here are a few of them.

First, the grace of the Lord is always sufficient, but it is temporary. Before you brand me as a heretic, let me explain what I mean. Many Christians like to claim this verse (2 Corinthians 12:9) out of its context. Paul was writing out of deep spiritual longing and confusion. He couldn't understand why a God of incomparable love and unlimited power wouldn't take away this "thorn in the flesh" that was giving him so much trouble. He never really got an answer, but he did discover the important truth that God's power is directly related to human weakness. Most of us simply want the pain to end and the weakness to be swallowed up in victory, but what if the entry point for an increase of God's power in our lives is that very thing that has broken us? God asked me, "Do you want my power to rest on you?" If so, I had to be willing to stay broken before Him. The well of God's grace is deep, but my bucket seems to be full of dents and holes that are caused by life's challenges. I have learned that these are not liabilities. They're the very things that keep me drawing from the well.

Second, the enemy of my soul wants to destroy my trust in God. If I see myself as a victim, then the underlying thought will be that God wasn't strong enough or didn't care enough to protect me. Let me be very clear on this point. Hardship is not spiritually neutral. It will either draw us closer to Jesus, or we will allow it to drive a wedge between us and our Father. John 6:44 tells us that one role of the Holy Spirit is to draw us to Jesus. If we let the Spirit work in our lives, He will keep us close to the Savior, and there we will discover love and safety that is not diminished by anything that can happen to us.

Finally, God often leads by closing doors, and closed doors can be painful. Just read Acts 16. Paul and his companions were the original Live Dead church-planting team! They were committed to taking the gospel where it didn't exist. They wanted to preach the good news in Asia, but they were kept from doing so by the Holy Spirit. The Holy Spirit actually closed the door. Why? Because He had even greater things in store for this little apostolic band. They were going to be the first to take the gospel to Europe. Miracles happened, many were saved, the church was established, persecution broke out, the apostles modeled Christlike joy in the face of hardship, and then they moved on to start it all over again. All of this could have been thwarted if they had allowed their hearts to become hard. Instead, they allowed God to toughen their skin while keeping their hearts soft.

We like it when the call includes longevity, but it's never our goal. It wasn't the goal of those early church planters, and it can't be ours. We aren't victims. We're radical followers of Jesus who will trust Him wherever and however He chooses to lead. This is your Acts 16 moment. Draw deep from God's grace, rejoice in your temporary sufferings, model for your children and those new believers what it means to live joyfully, and keep pushing on. There's another unreached people group out there with your name on it.

Blessings,

Mark

True accountability is only possible when we **VOLUNTARILY MAKE OURSELVES VULNERABLE** to others and to God *in relationship.*

— EDMUND HART

FAITH JOURNEY

STOP TWENTY

The Value of Accountability

EXTRAVAGANT DAILY TIME WITH JESUS

BY EDMUND HART

Our abiding time is a time of preparation, a time when we create the capacity in our spirits to hear the voice of God and understand His will. I approach my abiding time in the following way:

PRAYER

Prayer is the cornerstone of our relationship to God and the fountain from which we can draw the strength we need for the task to which God has called us. While we should be in an attitude of prayer throughout the day, I try to be intentional in my abiding time in a few areas:

- First, I praise God for who He is and what He has done in me and in my family. I spend five to ten minutes acknowledging His greatness, love, and authority over my life, the life of my family, and, radiating out from there, to the ends of the earth.
- There are aspects of my life and character that aren't what they should be. I take five to ten minutes to confess these to God and ask for His help in these areas.
- My family is always on my mind, and I pray for my children constantly, but in my abiding time I am more intentional in my prayers for them. I take a few minutes with each child, praying that God will reveal Himself to them in a special way and

that they will find a place of ministry and purpose in their schools and with their friends.

- I spend ten to fifteen minutes praying for those God has brought into our lives here. Most of the time I don't know how I should pray for them, so I pray in the Spirit, interceding for their salvation.
- Finally, I take a few minutes to thank God for what He will do this day and to once again praise Him for who He is.

BIBLE READING

I have spent many years in deep, analytical study of the biblical text. Whether in college, graduate school, or teaching ministry, much of my time with the Bible was spent digging deeply in narrow topics. I continue to study like this, but in recent years I have realized I need to allow the Bible to speak to me in different ways. I wanted the story of the Bible to have greater impact on me and to have more of the Word in me. Have you ever lain on the beach and let the waves roll in over you and felt the pull of the water? This is the feeling I am talking about. So in my abiding time, I try to take in large amounts of Scripture without fussing over details and rooting out questions.

An ancient tradition organizes the Old Testament into three major divisions: the Law, the Prophets, and the Writings. I read five chapters from each of these sections, plus one Psalm. I follow that up with five chapters from the Gospels (including Acts) and five chapters from the rest of the New Testament. This is a lot of reading, but I do not read from two books on the same day in any one

EDMUND HART

My wife, Sloane, and I grew up overseas as MKs—missionary kids. I was born and raised in East Africa, and Sloane spent most of her life in Austria. While my home—and heart—will always be in Africa, the Lord placed a burden on my soul long ago for the Middle East. Sloane and I took a long, winding path to get to the field, and sometimes it felt as if we would never make it. But after what seemed like an eternity in the U.S., including the births of all four of our children, we finally did arrive in the Middle East.

Sloane and I were raised to respect authority and to take responsibility for our actions. It wasn't always easy to submit to authority (and I didn't always do it), but the lessons I learned growing up have helped shape me. There have been times in my ministry where I felt a decision being made was wrong. Sometimes it turned out I was right and sometimes I was not. But I have found that being accountable to leadership is never wrong.

section. So if I have two or three chapters left in a book, I will not begin a new book in the same section that day.

My schedule gives me the benefit of different books from the Old Testament complementing my reading from the New Testament. This rotation has added depth and meaning to my New Testament reading. Often I will read from an Old Testament book and then be confronted with a quotation or reference to that very passage in my New Testament reading.

I keep a notebook handy to jot down verses I want to investigate later or thoughts that pop into my head as I read, but I try to not let it break the flow. My Bible reading usually takes sixty to ninety minutes.

SUPPLEMENTAL READING

I often read some of the more contemplative works of the early church, by authors such as Ignatius, Tertullian, Augustine, Aquinas, and others. Rather than analyzing their theology, I try just to soak in their spirituality.

PRAISE

My great love of music is coupled with an abysmal amount of musical talent, so I usually spend my praise time listening to music (ranging from Christian contemporary to old hymns to operatic overtures that put the Scriptures to music) and raising my hands in praise and prayer while I mouth the words or sing quietly in surrender to God.

VULNERABILITY IN RELATIONSHIPS

BY EDMUND HART

And they heard the sound of the LORD God walking in the garden in the cool of the day, and the man and his wife hid themselves from the presence of the LORD God among the trees of the garden. —GENESIS 3:8 (NRSV)

The definition of the word *accountable* is pretty straightforward. It simply means that we are in a position where we must make an account for our actions. In other words, we must answer for what we have done or said, whether good or bad. Looking at a biblical understanding of accountability, we see that neither the Old Testament nor the New Testament has a direct equivalent of "accountable," but the idea is there in many places. In the Old Testament, the concept of accountability mostly revolves around the responsibility that the Israelites have to follow the Law of Moses. The prophets are sent to the Israelites to remind them of their obligation and to hold them accountable for their lack of dedication to the Law.

In several places in the New Testament, Jesus indicates that God will hold people accountable for their actions. Paul also talks about accountability in language similar to the Old Testament, highlighting the Law as the standard by which the Israelites were to be measured and held accountable.

THE HEART OF ACCOUNTABILITY

God did not intend to simply create a system of accountability whereby the wicked or the guilty could be punished. In other words, punishment was not the desired outcome of accountability.

What lies at the heart of accountability is relationship. God desired to have relationship with His creation, with Adam and Eve. He gave them rules to follow for their own good, but it is apparent that the Lord wanted His relationship with mankind to be the filter through which these rules were understood. One of the results of Satan's lies to Adam and Eve is that they began to doubt the nature of their relationship with God. They had sinned, disobeyed God, and there was no way around it. But instead of throwing themselves on God's mercy, they hid from Him. In their confusion and guilt, and with a knowledge of their nakedness, they thought of their shame and their punishment. They had broken God's rule and they had to be punished.

Adam and Eve's realization of their guilt led them to view God's system of accountability as one of rules and punishment rather than one of relationship. But what makes a truly biblical understanding of accountability unique is its foundation in relationship and, specifically, God's desire to have relationship with His creation.

NO ACCOUNTABILITY WITHOUT VULNERABILITY

True accountability cannot come without vulnerability. This vulnerability can be forced or voluntary. We do not have a choice in whether we want the government to review our taxes; that is a vulnerability forced on us. But allowing others to know what we do and think in the private areas of our lives requires us to voluntarily make ourselves vulnerable to others. This can be difficult, as there is potential for embarrassment or shame with friends, colleagues, and even authority figures.

We see this in Genesis 3, where Adam and Eve hide from the shame of their vulnerability rather than embrace it and place it before God. They are ashamed of what they have done and how they see themselves. They are afraid of the punishment that will come if God finds out. The idea that these two humans could hide from the One who has just been described as the creator of the world and everything in it is laughable. Perhaps it is meant to be seen this way. But the desire to hide from our shame and pretend we can be kept from accountability is part of our fallen human nature.

The point is neither to condemn nor justify Adam and Eve but rather to admit that this is how we are conditioned to think about our shortcomings and our shame, which affects our willingness to be vulnerable with others. Allowing ourselves to be vulnerable and accountable for our actions and thoughts is very difficult. Yet this vulnerability is the cornerstone of any truly deep relationship.

Accountability is one of the characteristics that define Live Dead teams. Those wishing to be part of a Live Dead team must agree to being held accountable in all aspects of our lives. This can be seen as a forced vulnerability, but it is hoped that the benefits of accountability will instead make it something we embrace and offer willingly. It must also be borne in mind that none of it is meant to be a cold, sterile acceptance of a system, but rather a commitment to relationships with colleagues and authority figures as we work together to accomplish the task before us. Accountability, the way God intended it, is only possible when we voluntarily make ourselves vulnerable to others and to God in relationship.

What makes a truly biblical understanding of accountability unique is its foundation in relationship and, specifically, God's desire to have relationship with His creation.

— EDMUND HART

MEDITATIONS

The writer says, "At the heart of accountability is relationship. True accountability is only possible when we voluntarily make ourselves vulnerable to others and to God in relationship." Think of the ways you are accountable for what you say and do in your life.

To whom are you accountable in your day-to-day activities and your relationship with God? If you do not have an accountability partner or group, do you need one?

JOURNALING

1) List some areas of your life—including the things you say, think, and do—in which you need to be held accountable.

2) Find at least one Scripture verse relating to each of these areas. Then write out the verses in your journal.

ACCOUNTABILITY, PROFITABILITY, AND OUR DAILY LIVES

BY EDMUND HART

Obey your leaders, and submit to them; for they keep watch over your souls, as those who will give an account. Let them do this with joy and not with grief, for this would be unprofitable for you. —HEBREWS 13:17 (NASB)

I don't know how many times growing up I heard my parents tell me I was being disciplined for my own good. Deep down, I knew they were right and that I should accept it and learn from it. Of course, I didn't always do that, and it almost never felt good. But from an early age, I learned to respect both the authority of my parents and others and to see the value in accountability. The more areas of our lives that we open to accountability, the more benefit we will reap in our mental, physical, emotional, and spiritual health.

ACCOUNTABILITY IN OUR DAILY LIVES

One of the beautiful things about serving on a team is that it gives you an opportunity to allow accountability in your daily routine and activities. This is not a matter of giving up our freedoms and surrendering our privacy to the scrutiny of others. It is about recognizing that accountability extends to areas that we may not have considered before, including the following:

Accountability for our finances. This is more than the financial accountability and oversight that comes as part of being in an organization with procedures for tracking and reporting on expenditures. In the context of a church-planting team, this accountability goes beyond that to address the proper use of even our personal finances. The point is not to police what someone buys; we all have different tastes and value things differently. But it is easy to allow the material things of the world to distract us. Financial accountability gives us the best chance of being good stewards of God's resources and escaping the draw of material goods and the love of money.

Accountability for our physical health. I used to be athletic. At least I used to be able to play sports without getting winded or injured. Over time, the pressure of school, work, family, and ministry pushed my exercise time out of a place of priority, and, unfortunately, my eating habits did not change with my decrease in exercise. Ironically, the time I gained by skipping my exercise was less productive in the long run because I was tired and not nearly as energetic.

Lack of sleep, not enough exercise, bad diet—all of this can lead to sickness, ineffective work, and lost opportunities. Many times I have missed good opportunities for relationship building or even sharing the gospel because I was simply too tired. When we don't exercise or get enough sleep, we risk not being physically or mentally able to capitalize on opportunities that the Lord brings our way.

We have a duty to keep ourselves healthy for our families and for the sake of our work and calling. Being accountable to others can help ensure that we take the necessary steps to a healthy lifestyle.

Accountability for our family's health. Nobody likes being told how to be a better spouse or parent. But often, especially in a foreign culture, we are unable to see areas where we may need help when it comes to our families. Allowing our coworkers and leaders to hold us accountable for how we are maintaining our families and marriages can save us untold heartache.

ACCOUNTABILITY IN OUR SPIRITUAL LIVES

Slavery to religious ritual is abundant in the Arab world. The measure of religious devotion is tied to activities that can be seen and counted. Praying a certain number of times each day, fasting at the appropriate times, memorizing holy writings and teachings, and attending religious services all add up to a high level of "spirituality."

When we speak of accountability in our spiritual lives, we are thinking of something very different from this sort of public accounting. For us, spiritual accountability is about having people in our lives who help ensure we are growing in our relationship with God—not about a checklist confirming we have performed all the required religious duties.

Accountability in our spiritual lives extends beyond simply having somebody check up on how we are doing with our abiding time. After all, it would be easy for me to just say that I am doing well even if I am not. The other aspect of accountability comes in the fruit that we bear. How I interact with others and how I handle difficult situations exposes aspects of my spiritual condition. For example, if I am always aggressive, mean spirited, and bullying when I interact with others, that is a sign that things are probably not healthy in my spiritual life. The quality of our spiritual lives is directly related to the fruit we bear. The tree, after all, is known by its fruit (Matthew 12:33). Having accountability partners who can help us maintain purity in what we allow into our minds and out through our actions is increasingly essential in our modern age of anonymity.

ACCOUNTABILITY AND PROFITABILITY

The passage from Hebrews quoted at the beginning of this chapter makes a clear connection between our willingness to accept accountability and our own profit. Specifically it says that if we make it difficult for those in authority to hold us accountable, it will be "unprofitable" for us. Does this mean that causing grief for our overseers will cause us to miss out on some kind of reward?

I can remember as a teenager doing something inappropriate that got me grounded for a week. My friends had been planning a big party, and my grounding meant I would miss it. I was crushed and angry. I told my friends of my reversal in fortune, and, in a show of solidarity, they decided to reschedule the party for another time.

I couldn't wait to get home and tell my father that the party had been postponed and that his punishment was therefore rendered ineffectual. I figured he would probably threaten to ban me from the party whenever it was. But his response floored me. With a slight look of disappointment in his eyes, he simply said, "You should have better quality friends than that." I realized then (and continue to appreciate more and more) that my lack of acceptance of accountability wasn't simply about my missing or not missing a party. It was about not allowing my father to build character and responsibility into me. I wasn't missing a party, I was poisoning my future.

This is the essence of what the author of Hebrews is telling us. The word "unprofitable" here is the Greek word *alysiteles*, which has the sense of something that is unhelpful or harmful. In medical usage, it has the sense of something that can cause ill health. Fighting accountability won't simply result in a negative mark in our file, a slap on the wrist, or even a more serious punishment. The ultimate downside to resisting accountability is the damage it does to our character and spiritual condition. Of course, the implication of the passage is that our willing acceptance of accountability will have the positive result of building character.

ACCOUNTABILITY IN OUR CALLING

BY EDMUND HART

"If I say to the wicked, 'You shall surely die,' and you give them no warning, or speak to warn the wicked from their wicked way, in order to save their life, those wicked persons shall die for their iniquity; but their blood I will require at your hand." —EZEKIEL 3:18 (NRSV)

The Old Testament prophets were given some heavy assignments. Elijah took his life in his hands by condemning the actions of the king of Israel. Amos, a migrant farm worker and shepherd for hire, was required to announce God's judgment in the capital of Israel. Jeremiah was told to speak the truth about God's plans for Jerusalem, going against the king and his leaders and priests. Ezekiel was commanded to tell his own people, already crushed by defeat, that there was more on the way.

When I read their stories, I am often glad I was not one of these prophets. Yet we are called to a similar task. In the car one day, my six-year-old daughter asked me if we were prophets. When I asked her what she thought, she said she thought we were. She said the prophets were called to tell people what God wanted them to do and how they could better obey Him and become His friends again. She thought we were supposed to do the same thing. Sometimes children see things so simply and clearly.

The Lord held the prophets accountable for the task to which He called them, and that accountability in the calling extends to us.

ACCOUNTABLE FOR OUR PREPARATION

Abraham Lincoln is reported to have said that if he were given six hours to chop down a tree, he would spend the first four hours sharpening his axe. This has long been a favorite saying of mine—even if I haven't always lived up to its ideal. We want to be in a constant state of preparation so that we are not caught merely reacting to events or situations.

A story from the Gospel of Mark illustrates this well. Jesus often took time to be alone and to pray. In Mark 9, He takes a few of His disciples with Him to be alone. After coming back to the rest of the disciples in verse 14, He notices a crowd. A man with a demon-possessed son had come to the disciples requesting help, but they could not cast out the demon. Jesus restores the boy and the crowd disperses. When the disciples ask why they could not cast the demon out, Jesus replies, "This kind can be cast out only by prayer." Jesus is declaring that certain situations require more than reactionary prayer. It is unthinkable that the disciples did not pray when the man brought the boy to them. Jesus was saying they needed to follow His example and be prepared for such scenarios by taking time to get away, pray, and commune with God.

Our abiding time is where we become people who live in a state of preparation. We may not have any idea what is in store for us that day or week, but we have spent time in the presence of God and when we are confronted with situations we will not simply react to them but will be prepared for them. Ultimately, then, our accountability for our preparation comes in the form of how we handle the challenges and opportunities that come our way.

ACCOUNTABLE FOR OUR OPPORTUNITIES

All of us are given opportunities every day to do something significant for the Kingdom. It may not be explicit evangelism or even anything that will be noticed by others. A simple email of encouragement or a calm response to an angry person can be the key that unlocks a series of opportunities that lead to great things. In our part of the world, where direct evangelism is not always an option, taking advantage of opportunities is critical.

J. O. Savell, one of the early Assemblies of God leaders in Texas, once received a phone call from a man in a nearby hospital. Savell did not know the individual and asked how he had gotten his number. The man responded that he needed to talk to a minister but was not from the area, so he had prayed for God to help him find someone. The Lord put Savell's name in his mind, and the man looked up his number in the phonebook. After going to the hospital and praying with the man, Savell headed back to his car. Only then did the magnitude of the moment hit him: The man had called out to God in need, and the Lord had given him Savell's name.

People across the Arab world are crying out to God. They cannot go to a phonebook and look up the name of a local minister or church. They most likely don't even know a true Christian. Perhaps God will put the name of a believer in their mind and they will go to them. Or perhaps God will cause them to sit down next to one of us on the bus, in the park, or guide us to rent the empty apartment next to theirs. What will we do with these opportunities? Will we be prepared? Will we seize them with boldness? Or shy away out of fear, exhaustion, or lack of perception?

Being held accountable by our coworkers and leaders for our opportunities is not about condemnation and guilt. When I request prayer for the relationships I have developed, I know I will be prayed for and I know I will be asked about these relationships. Not only does this accountability create motivation within me to make the most of my interactions, but it also provides another set of spiritual eyes to help me see when these windows are opening.

ACCOUNTABLE FOR OUR WORK

In 1 Corinthians 3, Paul gives a compelling illustration of the importance of doing our work carefully and properly. When it comes to building the community of faith, various materials can be used. Some are costly and good, such as gold, silver, and jewels. Some are cheap and inferior, such as wood, hay, and straw. The point is not the expense of the materials but the durability. Those who build wisely with superior material will have their work pass through the time of testing and still stand. Those who do not build wisely and use inferior material will see their work burned up.

This passage is often taken as a statement on how we will be judged for our individual actions, but it really concerns the fate of communities of faith. What is at stake is the well-being and continued existence of the community and not simply a personal judgment of our work. If we build the community with inferior material, choosing not to follow Christ's plan because of a lack of preparation, laziness, or the desire for personal glory, the community will suffer. Trial and suffering will come to the community.

This is true anywhere in the world, but it's especially true in our area. In many of our countries, conversion to Christianity is against the law and comes with a heavy price. This is not the environment in which to engage in shoddy workmanship. Our work will be held accountable, through persecution, trial, and suffering. Will the communities that we help start and nurture survive their trials?

One thing is for sure: If we do not embrace accountability, we will increase the likelihood of making mistakes, building with inferior materials, and watching our communities be engulfed in flames. Ezekiel was not held responsible for how his fellow Israelites responded to his message, but he was held responsible for the message and the manner in which he delivered it.

All of us are given opportunities every day to do something significant for the Kingdom.

— EDMUND HART

JOHN WESLEY'S SELF-EXAMINATION QUIZ

Part of accountability is thoughtful contemplation and confession. More than 200 years ago, John Wesley gave nearly two dozen questions to his discipleship groups for this purpose. The questions originated from Wesley's spiritual accountability group he started when he was a student at Oxford. The group called themselves "The Holy Club." The first list appeared between 1729 and 1730 in the preface to Wesley's second Oxford diary. Similar questions appeared in his 1733 book called *A Collection of Forms of Prayer for Every Day in the Week.* As late as 1781, Wesley published this list of questions in the *Arminian Magazine.*[74]

Believers through the centuries have found great value in them and have used them as a platform for accountability. Write these questions in your journal and process them often with a community of believers.

1. Am I consciously or unconsciously creating the impression that I am better than I really am? In other words, am I a hypocrite?

2. Do I confidentially pass on to others what has been said to me in confidence?

3. Can I be trusted?

4. Am I a slave to dress, friends, work, or habits?

5. Am I self-conscious, self-pitying, or self-justifying?

6. Did the Bible live in me today?

7. Do I give the Bible time to speak to me every day?

8. Am I enjoying prayer?

9. When did I last speak to someone else of my faith?

10. Do I pray about the money I spend?

11. Do I get to bed on time and get up on time?

12. Do I disobey God in anything?

13. Do I insist upon doing something about which my conscience is uneasy?

14. Am I defeated in any part of my life?

15. Am I jealous, impure, critical, irritable, touchy, or distrustful?

16. How do I spend my spare time?

17. Am I proud?

18. Do I thank God that I am not as other people, especially as the Pharisees who despised the publican?

19. Is there anyone whom I fear, dislike, disown, criticize, hold a resentment toward, or disregard? If so, what am I doing about it?

20. Do I grumble or complain constantly?

21. Is Christ real to me?

MEDITATIONS

Reread John Wesley's Holy Club questions. Place a copy of the questions in a spot you see every day, such as your bathroom mirror, inside your car, or wherever you pray. Read and reflect on these questions daily, and track your thoughts in your journal. Visit this journal page often.

JOURNALING

1) Look through a newspaper or magazine for words or images that make you think of the way you desire to live your life.

2) Tear out these words and images and tape them into your journal or on your list of Wesley's Holy Club questions.

STOP TWENTY-ONE

A Walk Through Tunis

A WALK THROUGH TUNIS

O ur guest, Grace, landed two days ago. And now that she has adjusted to the surroundings, she's ready to explore. Chatting before her arrival, I discovered that Grace loves history and current events, exotic food and coffee. We have all of that in Tunis. Nearby Carthage was an important site in early Christianity, and more recently the protests in our own city sparked the Arab Spring. And then there's the Arabic coffee and local foods—no Starbucks or McDonald's to be found here.

"Where would you like to go first?" I ask.

"Take me to your favorite place," she says.

"I know exactly where we'll start."

"It's Sidi Bou Said," my husband, David, says. "It's always Sidi Bou Said."

Sidi Bou Said sits on a hill overlooking the sea and the rest of Tunis. It is the old part of the city, as the capital has extended its way up over the years. I tell Grace it's beautiful up there. It has an old-town feel—absolutely amazing. At night the city lights create a striking scene, and during the day we can see the gorgeous blue hues of the Mediterranean.

We set out, navigating Tunis's light-rail system, and make our way there. "This place looks familiar," Grace says as we get closer. "I feel like I'm in a wall calendar. You know the ones that feature cities on the Mediterranean?"

She's right—this part of the city is a tourist destination. All of the buildings feature the familiar white with blue window shades and blue trim. This area is also famous for its doors. They have some of the most uniquely colored and shaped wooden doors here. It's pretty common to see pictures of them everywhere.

We get off at the Sidi Bou Said stop and head for the streets closer to the sea. I want Grace to take in this view straightaway. As we reach the edge overlooking the sea, she says, "Okay, you win. This is beautiful. The water is so intensely blue." I pat myself on the back.

"Anyone interested in some coffee?" David asks. We're all in.

Along the way, men are selling souvenirs to tourists. We pass shops and booths full of paintings, pottery, clothing, birdcages—an assortment of trinkets. At the top of the hill is a coffee shop. Men are sitting outside, facing the street and watching the people walk by. We get our coffee and find a table near the front so we can also watch while we chat.

"How often do you come up here?" Grace asks.

"We'll come with friends at night or with visitors like you to have coffee and tea, and just talk and hang out, when there are fewer tourists around," I say. "I have a friend who lives up here, and we go up on her roof at night and drink tea and stare at the city lights."

I also come up here to hang out with my closest Tunisian friend, and I tell Grace her story: I met her on one of my first visits to the city, before I moved here. She was not a Christian yet, still a Muslim, and lived with her family. She became a believer about six months after I moved here, and her family kicked her out of their home. The only thing she was able to take was her backpack; her father took her papers and ID card.

She stayed with me that night, and I did my best to make her feel at home, offering basic things like shampoo and hair products. She cried and said, "No one has ever let me use their stuff like this." Our friendship solidified in those moments, and we eventually became roommates.

My friend had many ups and downs with her family. They wouldn't speak to her for a year. She fully embraced Christianity from the start and shared her faith with everyone around her. She was not afraid; she had no fear of police because her father was a police officer. She didn't understand until later that he was getting pressure about his daughter having become a Christian. And he, in turn, put pressure on her. Eventually they resolved things.

She worked really hard and never once compromised her faith. She got a job at the American school and worked her way up to admissions director. She shared with the Tunisian people in the school, including some radical people who threatened her, but she led many to the Lord. She's been interrogated at the Ministry of the Interior. They wanted her to sign papers denying she became a Christian and to become a Muslim again. She wouldn't. They asked why, and she shared the gospel with them.

"What a great story," Grace says. "I loved hearing it. Most of the stories in the States are doom and gloom, hate and violence. This is a story of salvation and perseverance."

She turns to David. "How about you? Any good stories?"

"Nothing like that one," he says.

"Tell the one about the sheep," I say.

"Oh, man. It's not as inspirational as yours."

"But it's a good picture of the culture."

"Okay, so I have been working with college students here," he says, "and there was one guy that I would meet for coffee. He was a very devout Muslim. The end of November that year was Eid, or the Feast of the Sacrifice, where Muslims remember Abraham's willingness to sacrifice Ishmael—a twist on the biblical account. Anyway, my friend invited me to join his family for the celebration. We left at 6 a.m. for the suburbs, and upon arriving they led me to their formal guest room with a couch and TV. They turned on the TV and let me sit there for a couple of hours while they prepared the meal.

"Eventually we went outside. I saw the sheep there ready to be slaughtered and a grill about the size of a cereal bowl with a small pile of coals. Some families have the butcher come to the house, and others just buy the meat, but this family was very traditional and slaughtered the sheep right there. It was a total of seventeen minutes from a live sheep to being grilled on this tiny grill.

"As their guest, they gave me the first piece of meat from the grill and proceeded to grill one piece at a time. The grill was so small you would get one piece of meat every twenty minutes. Then they told me they had a special piece for me—the tail—but thinking about it later, I think it was a slice of the brain. It was mushy and not good, but it was their way of honoring me, so I ate it."

Grace says, "Her story was inspirational, but yours was highly entertaining. It reminds me of stories from my crazy family."

"It does, doesn't it?" he says. "One thing that always pops into my mind is that the people here are just like everyone else I've lived around my whole life. When I first moved here, I thought of them as a completely different people, as if they were people I could never relate to. One day walking down the road, I started looking at faces and imagining them going to work or home to family. I would see a man in a suit and realize that he was probably working a twelve-hour day to provide for his family. It was then I could relate to them as people. Where first I saw foreigners, now I see neighbors."

In the Arab world,
there are more than
**350 UNREACHED
PEOPLE GROUPS**
made up of
300 MILLION SOULS.

— PETE &
WILMA GLASS

FAITH JOURNEY

STOP TWENTY-TWO

The Value of Pioneering

EXTRAVAGANT DAILY TIME WITH JESUS

BY WILMA GLASS

When I was a little girl growing up in a Christian home, I learned a Sunday school song that went like this: "Read your Bible, pray every day, and you you'll grow, grow, grow!" I believe it—and Pete and I practice it. Through our thirty-five years of marriage, we have made Bible reading and prayer the two bedrock essentials of our Christian walk.

Two Bible verses highlight the importance of Bible reading and prayer. The first is Matthew 4:4 (NKJV): "Man shall not live by bread alone, but by every word that proceeds from the mouth of God." We hear so much today about the benefits of healthy eating. As a result, we make an effort to carefully select fresh and nutritious foods in order to maintain good physical health. Excellent spiritual health requires determination and discipline, too. Pete and I try to take time every morning to read and discuss Scripture together.

Psalm 119:97-104 (MSG) sums up our love for God's Word: "Oh, how I love all you've revealed; I reverently ponder it all the day long. Your commands give me an edge on my enemies; they never become obsolete. I've even become smarter than my teachers since I've pondered and absorbed your counsel. I've become wiser than the wise old sages simply by doing what you tell me. I watch my step, avoiding the ditches and ruts of evil so I can spend all my time keeping your Word. I never make detours from the route you laid out; you gave me such good directions. Your words are so choice, so tasty; I prefer them to the best home cooking. With your instruction, I understand life; that's why I hate false propaganda."

Word breaks are more important to us than coffee breaks. We were recently at the site of ancient Caesarea, a town in Israel midway between Tel Aviv and Haifa. It was a great time for a Word break. We read the story in Acts 10 where Peter preached to the house of Cornelius at Caesarea. Earlier this year, we were at Saint Paul's Bay on the island of Malta—time for a Word break! We read from God's Word (Acts 27-28) the story of Paul's shipwreck on Malta.

The second verse that guides our abiding time is 1 Thessalonians 5:17-18 (NKJV): "Pray without ceasing, in everything give thanks; for this is the will of God in Christ Jesus for you." Constant prayer with thanksgiving is God's will for every follower of Christ. We begin and end our days with prayer, including large doses of praise and thanksgiving for all that God has done. I often start my day with music and some "worship aerobics" to get my heart really pumping for God. Then, throughout the day, we continue to pray about everything (Philippians 4:6).

Constant prayer with thanksgiving is God's will for every follower of Christ.

— PETE & WILMA GLASS

THE MOTIVATION OF PIONEERS

BY PETE & WILMA GLASS

We were ten and thirteen when we first heard the opening lines that would become so familiar. "Space: the final frontier. These are the voyages of the starship *Enterprise*. Its five-year mission: to explore strange new worlds, to seek out new life and new civilizations, to boldly go where no man has gone before."

We love adventure, so we tuned in to *Star Trek* week after week. That idea—boldly going where no man had gone before—became part of us.

Billions of people are still waiting to hear the gospel message for the first time. In the Arab world, there are more than 350 unreached people groups made up of 300 million souls. Pioneers are still needed to boldly go where no one has gone before—men and women of faith who will venture into unknown or unclaimed territory for Christ to plant the church where it does not yet exist.

For some, pioneering may sound glamorous. It might conjure up images of adventure, escape, exotic travel, risk, exploration. The pioneers of the Bible certainly experienced all of the above, but it is important that we draw a distinction here. We are not talking about Christian tourism—travel, adventure, living on the edge for a self-centered thrill. We are talking about a pioneering spirit that flows from full surrender to the lordship of Jesus Christ. We say, "I will go where *You* want me to go, dear Lord." It flows out of obedience to Jesus and His Great Commission: "Go into all the world and preach the gospel to all creation" (Mark 16:15).

WHAT MOTIVATES PIONEERS?

Why do God's pioneers do what they do? What motivates them? One of the first pioneers of the Bible was Abraham. As you read his story, beginning in Genesis 12, you see a great example of a pioneer compelled by faith and obedience.

After clearly hearing from God, he packs up his tents, family, and belongings and heads into the unknown on a journey of faith with God. Like Abraham, pioneers are willing to go wherever God sends them. That is what pioneers do. Pioneers are always advancing.

A team of pioneers working among an unreached people group in the Himalayas recently sent out a report that included this statement: "But knowing that God had sent us, we went in with a 'do it or die trying' attitude. And now our 'foolishness' is starting to bear fruit. Pretty exciting stuff."

Did you catch it? "Knowing that God had sent us"—that is key. That is what makes all the difference. When we know that God is telling us to go, nothing can stand in our way. We can imagine the words of the doubters: "Ah, Abraham, consider the dangers! You cannot cross the desert or go into a new country without facing perils or sword. You could encounter robbers or armies. How will you live?" To this, we can also hear Abraham's response: "He will supply. He who bids me go must take the responsibility of that upon Himself. He will care for us."

Hebrews 13:5 (MSG) instructs us: "Don't be obsessed with getting more material things. Be relaxed with what you have. Since God assured us, 'I'll never let you down, never walk off and leave you,' we can boldly quote, 'God is there, ready to help; I'm fearless no matter what. Who or what can get to me?' "

We see these same ideas expressed in the life of the apostle Paul and his church-planting team (Acts 16:6-10). After Paul sees a vision of a man in Macedonia calling for help, we read, "After he had seen the vision, immediately we sought to go to

Macedonia, concluding that the Lord had called us to preach the gospel to them" (Acts 16:10 NKJV). They knew God had called them to go to a certain people and place, and so they went.

God continues to call His servants today. But why would you want to leave the United States to live somewhere in the Arab world? After all, you've won the lottery! You're living the dream. Many of our friends in the Arab world would give their right arms for the chance to move to America, the land of opportunity. We'll never forget first arriving in Casablanca with our two little blond-haired children. Our new Moroccan neighbors were amazed that we would choose to live in North Africa. They, after all, dreamed of living in America. Why were we there? Adventure? Travel? Thrills? No. We knew that God had sent us.

But as in the days of Jesus, the workers are few. In the world today, 3.5 billion people are Muslim, Hindu, or Buddhist—and 86 percent of them do not know a follower of Christ. Of the 100,000 missionaries serving around the world, only about 3 percent work among unreached people groups. In Luke 10:2, Jesus says, "The harvest is plentiful, but the workers are few. Ask the Lord of the harvest, therefore, to send out workers into his harvest field." Please pause right now and ask the Lord to send more workers.

More pioneers are needed to go where He wants them to go. We believe, in these end times, that God is summoning the whole church to join in the unfinished work of taking the gospel to those who have not yet heard. As Hudson Taylor put it, "The Great Commission is not an option to be considered; it is a command to be obeyed."

Our motivation must begin with His Word, and He has clearly spoken. His will and priorities are revealed in the Bible: "Therefore go and make disciples of all nations, baptizing them in the name of the Father and of the Son and of the Holy Spirit" (Matthew 28:19).

John Piper writes: "God is pursuing with omnipotent passion a worldwide purpose of gathering joyful worshipers for Himself from every tribe and tongue and people and nation. He has an inexhaustible enthusiasm for the supremacy of His name among the nations. Therefore, let us bring our affections into line with His, and, for the sake of His name, let us renounce the quest for worldly comforts and join His global purpose."

"By faith Abraham obeyed when he was called to go out to the place which he would receive as an inheritance," (Hebrews 11:8 NKJV). He obeyed. He obeyed. He obeyed. We too must obey God. The people of our world living in spiritual darkness will not be reached with the light of the gospel without Christ followers who, like Abraham, obey God and go. We must die to ourselves, to our own will and plans. We must demonstrate a total surrender to the lordship of Jesus and His priorities.

Pioneers are going where others aren't going or can't go, to engage people groups who have never before heard the gospel of Jesus. This is why we do what we do. This is our motivation. "Then I heard the voice of the LORD saying, 'Whom shall I send? And who will go for us?' And I said, 'Here am I. Send me!' " (Isaiah 6:8).

MEDITATIONS

If you are motivated to leave the United States and live in the Arab world, what is your motivation to do so? Journal about it.

_____

_____

_____

_____

_____

_____

_____

_____

_____

_____

THE DESTINATION OF PIONEERS

BY PETE GLASS

"Do you not say, 'There are yet four months, and then comes the harvest'? Behold, I say to you, lift up your eyes and look on the fields, that they are white for harvest." —JOHN 4:35 (NASB)

Where does the church not exist? Where are the unengaged? These are questions asked by pioneers, following the example of Paul: "It has always been my ambition to preach the gospel where Christ was not known" (Romans 15:20). Pioneers are propelled by possibility. They are always looking ahead, thinking about "out there," just a little farther. Paul's conception of frontier missions was one of constantly pressing beyond where the church was established to places where there was no witness to Christ.

Some imagine that the work of taking the gospel to the ends of the earth is just about wrapped up. Nothing could be farther from the truth. More than 40 percent of the people groups of the world are still considered unreached. The Great Commission to make disciples of all nations is still in effect. And since there are thousands of nations—ethnolinguistic people groups—today who have never heard of Him, every Christ follower should pray that God would not only make all of us evangelists among our own people, but also that He would raise up from among us pioneers to take the gospel where it has never gone before.

I lived in Dallas for two years while studying Bible and theology at Christ for the Nations Bible Institute. While living there, I worked as a waiter in a chic downtown Cajun French restaurant. Six of the other waiters were Moroccans. I soon learned from them that all Moroccans are Muslim—or so they thought. I grew up in Sheboygan, Wisconsin, and lived there from birth until I went away to college. I had never met a Moroccan and knew nothing at all about Morocco or Islam. But working in that restaurant, the Moroccans and I became close friends. I would often see them slip out to a side room, near the restaurant kitchen, where they would kneel together in a line to do their prayers. I grew curious and was soon reading everything I could get my hands on to better understand the faith of my new friends.

Wilma and I began to spend more time talking and reading about Islam, Muslims, and North Africa. We began to dream about visiting Morocco someday and started looking for opportunities. Little by little, we were lifting our eyes to the fields. In the days that followed, we both began to feel that God might be calling us to live and work in Morocco.

PETE & WILMA GLASS

Since surrendering our lives to Christ as students in the early '70s, we've been on a nonstop adventure with Jesus. We grew up in God's country—Wisconsin—and got married in 1977. We have two grown children and three grandchildren: Max, Jack, and Lily.

Soon after we began our life together, we discovered that we are church planters at heart. God has given us the incredible privilege of pioneering churches in Wisconsin and in North Africa. North Africa is Muslim territory, a difficult place to be a Christian and a dangerous place for those who dare to share the gospel and for those who would convert to Christianity.

We started out in Morocco in 1987 and relocated to Tunisia in 2011. We love North Africans, the majority of whom are Muslims. Here in North Africa, we need pioneers. The apostle Paul was a pioneer. He was one who always pressed ahead to places where the gospel had not yet been proclaimed and the church had not yet been established. In Romans 15:20, he writes, "It has always been my ambition to preach the gospel where Christ was not known." Christ is still unknown to millions of Muslims across North Africa.

Eventually, we decided to contact Assemblies of God World Missions. We knew AGWM had missionaries stationed around the world, so we thought perhaps they could link us up with some workers in North Africa. So I called the AGWM office, gave a brief introduction, and explained that Wilma and I believed God was calling us to North Africa and in particular to Morocco. I asked if they could help by putting us in touch with an Assemblies of God missionary working in Morocco or elsewhere in North Africa. The answer I was given was short and sweet: "We have none."

Not long after I made that phone call, the Iran hostage crisis took center stage in world news. For 444 days, from November 1979 to January 1981, fifty-two Americans were held hostage by Islamist militants inside the U.S. embassy in Tehran. For the first time, we were exposed to images of chanting mobs of Iranian Muslims shouting "Death to America!" President Carter called the hostages "victims of terrorism and anarchy." More than once during those weeks, we asked God, *Are you really sure you are calling us to work among Muslims?* Looking back now, we can see how God was opening our eyes to a people and a part of the world we previously knew very little about. He was enlarging our vision of the harvest fields.

John 4 records a teaching of Jesus that reveals great insights for pioneers, especially the idea of lifting our eyes and looking on the fields. While His disciples are away searching for food, Jesus strikes up a conversation with a Samaritan woman at a well.

First, you need to know that Samaritans were literally despised by the Jews. Tensions between the Jews and Samaritans dated back well into the Old Testament period. Jewish and Samaritan religious leaders taught that it was wrong to have any contact with the opposite group, and neither was to enter the other's territories. So you can imagine the disciples' surprise when they return with the food and find Jesus talking with a woman—in itself a cultural taboo—not to mention that she is also one of those detestable Samaritans.

After her encounter with Jesus, the woman leaves them and her water jar and goes back to her town to tell everyone, "Come, see a man who told me everything I ever did. Could this be the Messiah?" (John 4:29). The people flock out to see for themselves.

Now with the Samaritans encircling them, Jesus speaks these words to His disciples: "Lift up your eyes and look on the fields" (John 4:35 NASB). The fields in this case were clearly all the Samaritan people surrounding them. Maybe it was scary. I'm sure the thought of Samaritans being included in the harvest plan had not yet crossed the minds of the disciples. Just a few lines down in the text, we read in verse 39, "Many of the Samaritans from that town believed in him," and again in verse 41, "And because of his words many more became believers." For Jesus' Jewish disciples, it must have been a stretch to lift up their eyes toward the Samaritans and to see them as being included in Jesus' harvest plan. I'm sure the disciples were blown away as they witnessed so many Samaritans believing in Jesus.

For many Christians today, the thought of moving to an Arab country to live among Muslims so that they might hear the gospel is also quite a stretch. It was for us. But this is what pioneers do.

So here's the point. Begin lifting up your eyes today and take a fresh look at the fields. Be sure to ask, *Where are the unengaged, least-engaged, and unreached fields of our world? Where is there no church?* The Arab world is made up of 300 million people, and very few pioneers are on the ground engaged in the work of proclaiming the gospel and planting the church where it does not exist.

Ask God to help you lift your eyes for a fresh look at the peoples of the world who are waiting to hear the gospel for the very first time. It's their turn.

THE DEVOTION OF PIONEERS

BY PETE & WILMA GLASS

For to me, to live is Christ and to die is gain. —PHILIPPIANS 1:21

Pioneers are devoted to the heart of God. They live and breathe for the glory of God, driven by throne interests and the advancement of His Kingdom. They live with a sort of reckless abandonment to His will because they love God with all of their heart, soul, mind, and strength and desire to serve Him because of this great love.

The story of David's mighty men is a great example of the kind of devotion we should have for Christ and His Kingdom. In 2 Samuel 23:8-39, we find a core group of faithful friends who served King David on the battle field with total allegiance. These men were mighty in valor and faith. They were not afraid to risk or to sacrifice, living for a purpose greater than themselves. They fearlessly offered their lives for their king. Why? Love. They loved their king more than life itself and in so doing, are examples to us of what our relationship to our Lord and King, Jesus Christ, ought to be.

My spirit is stirred especially by the devotion of David's men in verses 13-17: "During harvest time, three of the thirty chief warriors came down to David at the cave of Adullam, while a band of Philistines was encamped in the Valley of Rephaim. At that time David was in the stronghold, and the Philistine garrison was at Bethlehem. David longed for water and said, 'Oh, that someone would get me a drink of water from the well near the gate of Bethlehem!' So the three mighty warriors broke through the Philistine lines, drew water from the well near the gate of Bethlehem and carried it back to David. But he refused to drink it; instead, he poured it out before the LORD. 'Far be it from me, LORD, to do this!' he said. 'Is it not the blood of men who went at the risk of their lives?' And David would not drink it. Such were the exploits of the three mighty warriors."

In this account, David had hidden in the cave at Adullam because Saul was trying to kill him. The valley of Rephaim was near David's hometown of Bethlehem, where some Philistine soldiers—other enemies of David—had invaded and were living. Like many of us when we are away from home, we long for the things we miss. In David's case, it was the good, cold water of Bethlehem. Three of David's men were especially brave, loyal, and unselfish. They loved David, even risking their own lives to get him some water. This was not a simple task. Bethlehem was about twelve miles away past enemy troops. They had to fight the Philistines to get the water and walk all the way back again. In spite of these obstacles, their love for David was so strong that pleasing him was all that mattered to them. David's life and the throne were in their hands and they knew it. There was no risk too great.

In the world today, 3.5 billion people are Muslim, Hindu, or Buddhist—and 86 percent of them do not know a follower of Christ. Of the 100,000 missionaries serving around the world, only about 3 percent work among unreached people groups.

However, when David realized the sacrifice his men had made, just to get him water, he knew that no human king deserved this kind of loyalty. Only the Lord God Almighty deserves devotion such as this.

Are we devoted, loyal, and obedient to the King of Kings and Lord of Lords? He sacrificed Himself for us, giving us the gift of salvation and forgiveness of sins. Does He deserve any less than total devotion? Do we love our King Jesus so much that pleasing Him is all that matters? Are we so earnestly attached to Jesus and dedicated to His cause?

"And Jesus came and spake unto them, saying, All power is given unto me in heaven and in earth. Go ye therefore, and teach all nations, baptizing them in the name of the Father, and of the Son, and of the Holy Ghost: Teaching them to observe all things whatsoever I have commanded you: and, lo, I am with you always, even unto the end of the world. Amen" (Matthew 28:18-20 KJV).

His goal is that none should perish. There is no Plan B. It is our duty to be co-laborers in Christ. Like David's mighty men, we must live to please the King, putting our love for King Jesus above our own lives.

"Jesus said unto him, Thou shalt love the Lord thy God with all thy heart, and with all thy soul, and with all thy mind. This is the first and great commandment. And the second is like unto it, Thou shalt love thy neighbor as thyself. On these two commandments hang all the law and the prophets" (Matthew 22:37-40 KJV). Are the things that are important to Him important to us? Do we really love others because He first loved us? The greatest way to love your neighbor is by sharing the love of Jesus with him. Do we embrace the Great Commission and make it a priority in our prayers, finances, and actions?

The obedience that He is calling us to is not a life of purposeless suffering. No, He has promised to give us a future and a hope (Jeremiah 29:11). We are on the winning side! People from every tribe and language and people and nation will respond (Revelation 5:19).

Now the only question is whether you will be one of His "mighty men" or not. Our Lord still needs faithful men and women who will serve Him. We too are fighting a battle with our Lord, in the power of His strength and might, under the direction of the Holy Spirit. It is the battle for souls that are enslaved by our enemy, Satan. Will you determine today to be one of His "mighty men"?

MEDITATIONS

Are you considering working in the Arab world as a missionary? If so, where would you go to engage unreached people? Take some time to listen to the voice of the Holy Spirit.

JOURNALING

1) Find a small map of the Arab world online and print it out.

2) Place or tape the map in your journal.

3) In bright colors, fill in the countries or identify the cities that you feel drawn to pray for or visit.

4) Pray that God will call pioneers to these unreached areas.

FAITH JOURNEY

STOP TWENTY-THREE

Living and Dying Daily for the Pleasure of the One

313313

LIVING AND DYING DAILY FOR THE PLEASURE OF THE ONE

BY DICK BROGDEN

Pioneer work can be lonely and unrewarding at times. We know we're doing what the Lord desires, but we're human. Sometimes our desire for human encouragement and results gets in the way of our quest to "live for the pleasure of the One."

Scripture tells us one man plants and another waters, but God brings the increase. We believe this, but sometimes people serving in the Muslim world feel like they aren't even sowing seed, as the field is so full of rocks. Digging in this hard soil can be painful and requires determination to do what God wants, no matter the costs.

Of course, we aren't the first to do this kind of work. We stand high on the shoulders of the great pioneers who came before us. Many have found great comfort and encouragement through the years in the pages of Oswald Chambers's *My Utmost for His Highest*,[75] but did you know this? He is buried in Egypt, where he served from 1915 until his death two years later at the age of 43.

Another pioneer in Egypt was Lillian Trasher. "Mama Lillian" sailed to Egypt in 1910 with less than $100 in her pocket. She remained single and lived in Egypt until 1961, when she went home to be with "the father to the fatherless and the husband to the widow." She captured the heart of pioneering this way:

My work reminds me of the fable of a little boy who was crossing the desert alone. He became very thirsty, so he was obliged to dig in the ground with bleeding fingers until he came to water. He drank and went on his weary way. Each time he became thirsty he dug holes, and his hands became more torn and bleeding. At last he reached the other side, exhausted and fainting, his clothes hanging in dusty rags.

Some months later he looked across the desert and saw a happy little boy coming with his hands full of fresh flowers. The child was coming the very same way he had traveled. He looked at the strange sight in perfect amazement. When the little boy arrived, he asked him how it could be that he had crossed the awful desert and looked so fresh and cool.

The child answered, saying, "Oh, the way is beautiful. There are many small wells out of which spring lovely cool water, and around each of these wells there are flowers and shady bushes and soft green grass. I had no trouble at all in crossing."

The first boy looked down at his own scarred fingers and knew that it was his suffering which had made the desert bloom and had made the way easy for other little boys to cross. But no one would ever know to thank him or to ask who had dug the wells. But, he knew, and was satisfied.[76]

In whom do you find your satisfaction? Let's live and die for "the pleasure of the One."

Scripture tells us one man plants and another waters, but God brings the increase.

you just experienced is an introduction to the values that undergird the Live Dead movement set in the context of the Arab world. The principles derived are applicable everywhere—as increasingly are the Arabs. Arabs are immigrating into North America, Europe, and other nations around the world. God is sending some of us to work among the Arabs and bringing some of the Arabs to our suburbs that we might work among them at home. It is our prayer that this Journey has moved your heart to see Arabs as God sees them, to break your heart that they may come to know Jesus.

HOW DOES LIVE DEAD WORK IN THE ARAB WORLD?

If your heart has been moved for Arab Muslims and you feel God might be calling you to live and die among precious unreached peoples in the Arab world, we would love to connect with you. If you are American and not affiliated with a mission organization, we ask that you apply to Assemblies of God World Missions at goag.org (Assemblies of God leads but does not own Live Dead; we intentionally want to cooperate with other likeminded agencies). If you are American and affiliated with a sending agency or a non-American, please have your agency leaders contact us at arabworld@live-dead.org.

HOW YOU CAN GET INVOLVED IN LIVE DEAD ARAB WORLD

If *Live Dead The Journey* has given you a burden for the Arab world but you don't feel called to go, you are just as important to us and to Live Dead. You can help in several key ways:

1   INTERCESSION: On our website (arabworld.live-dead.org), you can sign up for updates by email, Facebook, or Twitter and subscribe to our blog. All of our social media is geared toward helping you to pray.

2   ADVOCACY: We are interested in mobilizing individuals and churches that will adopt one of our church-planting teams and help to raise up prayer, workers, and resources for those teams. More information can be found on the advocacy page of the website (arabworld.live-dead.org) or through our director of advocacy at advocacy@arabworld.live-dead.org.

3   PRAYER AND VISION TRIPS: Six to ten days in the Arab world can also be organized by contacting advocacy@arabworld.live-dead.org.

ENDNOTES

1 Harold Sala, *Heroes: People Who Made a Difference in Our World* (Uhrichsville, OH: Barbour Publishing, 1998).

2 Ibid.

3 Ibid

4 Ruth Tucker, *From Jerusalem to Irian Jaya: A Biographical History of Christian Missions* (Grand Rapids, MI: Zondervan, 2004), 170–175.

5 Joseph Thayer, *Thayer's Greek-English Lexicon of the New Testament: Coded with Strong's Concordance Numbers* (Peabody, MA: Hendrickson Publishers, 1996).

6 V. Raymond Edman, *The Disciplines of Life* (Colorado Springs, CO: Victor Books, 1975), and F. J. Heugel, *Bone of His Bone* (Jacksonville, FL: Seed Sowers Christian Books Publishing House, 1997).

7 Mark Edwards, *John Through the Centuries* in Blackwell Bible Commentaries (Oxford, UK: Wiley-Blackwell, 2004), 146–163.

8 John Piper, *A Holy Ambition: To Preach Where Christ Has Not Been Named* (Minneapolis, MN: Desiring God Ministries, 2011).

9 Ibid.

10 Daniel Sinclair, *A Vision of the Possible: Pioneer Church Planting in Teams* (Downers Grove, IL: IVP Books, 2012), 55.

11 A.W. Tozer, *The Best of A.W. Tozer*, Book 2 (Camp Hill, PA: Wingspread Publishers, 2007).

12 Sinclair, *A Vision of the Possible*, 33.

13 Ibid., 29.

14 David Platt, *Radical: Taking Back Your Faith from the American Dream* (Colorado Springs, CO: Multnomah Books, 2010), 64.

15 Charles H. Spurgeon, *2,200 Quotations from the Writings of Charles H. Spurgeon: Arranged Topically or Textually & Indexed by Subject, Scripture, and People* (Grand Rapids, MI: Baker Books, 1996).

16 Patrick Lencioni, *The Five Dysfunctions of a Team: A Leadership Fable* (Hobokin, NJ: Jossey-Bass, 2002), 217.

17 Sinclair, *A Vision of the Possible*, 39.

18 Oswald J. Smith, *The Passion for Souls* (Perrysburg, OH: Welch Publishing Co., 1986).

19 Jason Mandryk, *Operation World: The Definitive Prayer Guide to Every Nation* (Grand Rapids, MI: IVP Books, 2012).

20 *The Book of Common Prayer*, intro. James Wood (New York, NY: Penguin Classics, 2012).

21 Gordon Fee, *The First Epistle to the Corinthians* in The New International Commentary on the New Testament (Grand Rapids, MI: Eerdmans, Pub. Co, 1987), 397.

22 George Eldon Ladd, *A Theology of the New Testament* (Grand Rapids, MI: Eerdmans, Pub. Co., 1993). 388–420.

23 Alan R. Johnson, *Apostolic Function in 21st Century Missions* (Pasadena, CA: William Carey Library, 2009).

24 Mark 3:14, 6:6-12; Matthew 10:5-9; Luke 9:1-6

25 Acts 1:8

26 The believers in Jerusalem are called collectively the church in Acts 5:11, 8:1, 3, and 11:22. More broadly there is reference to the "church in Judea" in Acts 9:31.

27 Acts 8:4-8

28 Acts 8:25

29 Acts 10:27-48

30 Acts 11:19-21

31 See Acts 16:40-41 for churches in Syria and Cilicia; Acts 14:23 for churches formed on his first missionary journey out of Antioch in Galatia and Phrygia; and Acts 16, Philippi; Acts 17, Thessalonica and Berea; Acts 18, Corinth; and Acts 19-20 for Ephesus.

32 Acts 15:41

33 Acts 18:23

34 1 Timothy 2:7; 2 Timothy 1:11

35 2 Timothy 2:2

36 Titus 2:1

37 1 Corinthians 11:2; Philippians 4:9;
Colossians 3:7; 1 Thessalonians 4:1-2

38 Matthew 4:19

39 Mark 3:14-15

40 Luke 9:1-6, 10:1-12

41 John 15:1-8

42 John 14:12

43 Acts 4:33

44 Acts 5:12

45 Stephen, Acts 6:8; Philip, Acts 8:4-8

46 See Acts 13:9-11; a generic report of signs and
wonders in 14:3; a report of extraordinary miracles
through Paul in 14:8-10, 19:11; 20:10; and Paul's
own reflections in Romans 15:19;
1 Corinthians 2:1-4; 2 Corinthians 12:12.

47 F. F. Bruce, *The Book of Acts,* in The New
International Commentary on the New Testament
(Grand Rapids, MI: Eerdmans Publishing
Company, 1988), 13.

48 C. W. Carter, "Apostolic Age," in *Zondervan Pictorial
Encyclopedia of the Bible,* ed. Merrill C. Tenney (Grand
Rapids, MI: Zondervan, 1975), 97.

49 Ibid.

50 Acts 4:3-22

51 Acts 5:18

52 Acts 5:19

53 Acts 5:26

54 Acts 5:40

55 Acts 9:23

56 Acts 9:29-30

57 Acts 12:2

58 Acts 12:6-11

59 There is abusive talk against the preaching in
13:44, 14:2, 17:13; persecution in 13:50; stoning in
14:19; jail and flogging in 16:19-24; rioting in 17:5,
19:23-41; bringing Paul to court in 18:12-13; and
finally his arrest in Jerusalem, imprisonment, and
trip to Rome in the final chapters of Acts.

60 Romans 15:31; 1 Corinthians 2:1-4, 16:8;
2 Corinthians 1:8-11; his long list of hardships
in 2 Corinthians 6:3-10 and 11:21b-29;
1 Thessalonians 2:1-2; 2 Timothy 2:9

61 1 Corinthians 4:8-13

62 Acts 2:42

63 Galatians 2:10

64 1 Corinthians 16:1-4

65 1 Timothy 5:3-16

66 Ralph D. Winter, ed., *Perspectives on the World
Christian Movement: A Reader* (Pasadena, CA:
William Carey Library Publishers, 2009).

67 Bryant Myers, *Walking with the Poor: Principles and
Practices of Transformational Development* (Maryknoll,
NY: Orbis Books, 2011), 127.

68 Ibid., xxiv.

69 O. N. Muchena, "Sociological and
Anthropological Reflections." In T. Yamamori, B.
L. Myers, K. Bediako and L. Reed. eds. *Serving with
the Poor in Africa: Case Studies in Holistic Ministry.*
Monrovia, CA: MARC, 1996.

70 *The Book of Common Prayer.*

71 Elisabeth Elliot, *Shadow of the Almighty: The
Life and Testament of Jim Elliot* (New York, NY:
HarperCollins, 1989), 248.

72 Samuel Zwemer, "The Glory of the Impossible," in
Perspectives on the World Christian Movement.

73 Jean Pierre de Caussade, *Abandonment to Divine
Providence* (Harrisburg, PA: Trinity Press, 2013).

74 John Wesley, "A Scheme of Self-Examination Used
by the First Methodists in Oxford" in *The Works of
John Wesley,* ed. Thomas Jackson (Grand Rapids,
MI: Baker Book House, 1978), 521–523.

75 Oswald Chambers, *My Utmost for His Highest*
(Grand Rapids, MI: Discovery House Pub., 1992).

76 Janet and Geoff Benge, *Lillian Trasher: The
Greatest Wonder in Egypt* (Seattle, WA: YWAM
Publishing, 2003).

SUGGESTED READING LIST
FOR EXTRAVAGANT DAILY TIMES WITH JESUS

OSWALD CHAMBERS
My Utmost for His Highest
If You Will Ask: Reflections on the Power of Prayer

FRANCIS CHAN
Crazy Love: Overwhelmed by a Relentless God
Multiply: Disciples Making Disciples
Forgotten God: Reversing Our Tragic Neglect of the Holy Spirit

GENE EDWARDS
The Divine Romance
A Tale of Three Kings
Living Close to God
Revolution: The Story of the Early Church

JOHN ELDREDGE
The Utter Relief of Holiness: How God's Goodness Frees Us from Everything that Plagues Us
Beautiful Outlaw: Experiencing the Playful, Disruptive, Extravagant Personality of Jesus
Epic: The Story God Is Telling
Desire: The Journey We Must Take to Find the Love God Offers

FRANÇOIS FÉNELON
The Seeking Heart
The Inner Life
Talking with God

RICHARD FOSTER
Longing for God: Seven Paths of Christian Devotion
Celebration of Discipline: The Path to Spiritual Growth
Prayer: Finding the Heart's True Home
Sanctuary of the Soul: Journey into Meditative Prayer
Life with God: Reading the Bible for Spiritual Transformation

CHRISTOPHER HEUERTZ
Unexpected Gifts: Discovering the Way of Community
Friendship at the Margins: Discovering Mutuality in Service and Missions
Simple Spirituality: Learning to See God in a Broken World

C. S. LEWIS

A Year with C. S. Lewis: Daily Readings from His Classic Works

Mere Christianity

Reflections on the Psalms

Miracles

CALVIN MILLER

Into the Depths of God: Where Eyes See the Invisible, Ears Hear the Inaudible, and Minds Conceive the Unconceivable

The Disciplined Life

Loving God Up Close: Rekindling Your Relationship with the Holy Spirit

A Hunger for the Holy: Nurturing Intimacy with Christ

WANG MING-DAO

A Call to the Church

A Stone Made Smooth

JOHN PIPER

The Pursuit of God

Future Grace

Risk Is Right: Better to Lose Your Life than to Waste It

Think: The Life of the Mind and the Love of God

A Hunger for God: Desiring God Through Fasting and Prayer

Future Grace: The Purifying Power of the Promises of God

Let the Nations Be Glad: The Supremacy of God in Missions

CORRIE TEN BOOM

The Hiding Place

Amazing Love: True Stories of the Power of Forgiveness

I Stand at the Door and Knock: Meditations by Corrie ten Boom

A. W. TOZER

The Pursuit of God

The Knowledge of the Holy

God's Pursuit of Man

Man, the Dwelling Place of God

The Purpose of Man

Mornings with Tozer: A 366 Day Devotional

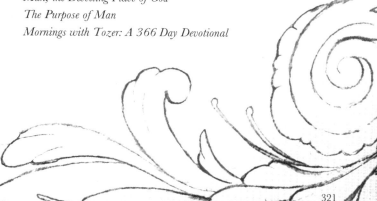

ABOUT THE COLLABORATORS

Mark Renfroe and his wife, Amy, have served in the Arab world for more than twenty years. They have four wonderful children—Noor, Habeeb, Nabil, and Emad. When asked why they gave them Arabic names, Mark and Amy's answer is simple: "When God called us to the Arab world, He gave us heart transplants. He gave us the heart of an Arab man and woman. After all, you can't really reach people you don't love." Mark surrendered to the grace of God at the age of twenty-two, and the one thing that keeps him going is the indescribable love of God that was ultimately demonstrated through the cross.

Dick Brogden and his wife, Jennifer, have been treasuring Jesus among Muslims in Mauritania (1992), Kenya (1993-95), Sudan (1995-2011), and North Africa (since 2011). Their two sons, Luke and Zack, were born in Sudan and consider themselves Africans. The Brogdens love Jesus with all their broken hearts and long that every ancient gate may be lifted up that Jesus, strong and mighty, King of Glory, may come in. They believe that God is best glorified in mission when His people work in multinational teams to reach the unreached and to plant the church where Christ has not been named.

Mike Murray and his wife, Nikki, have served among the Muslim people groups of Central Eurasia since 2006. They are committed to church planting in teams among the unreached. Prior to their appointment with Assemblies of God World Missions, Mike worked for ten years as a magazine editor and newspaper reporter. He now serves as editor of *Desert Rain,* the official magazine of the Live Dead network. Mike and Nikki have three children: Anna, Evan, and Colin.

Charity Reeb is a brand and marketing strategist with a heart to inspire people to go out and be Jesus' hands and feet to the unreached world. She is passionate about using the arts to communicate stories in a relevant way. Charity and her husband, Jeff, live in Springfield, Missouri, and travel to some of the world's most remote and lost locations to meet people, work with missionaries, and tell stories through campaigns such as Live Dead.

After spending most of his life traveling throughout the United States, ***Austin Evans*** now lives in Springfield, Missouri, where he raises his daughter and co-owns Transformation Gallery & Tattoo. Although Austin has always been deeply involved in art, and has been tattooing since 2006, it was not until recently that he realized God's call on his life to spread the love of Christ through his artwork. He spends his free time painting and raising his daughter with the knowledge of the love, power, and sacrifice of Christ.

Gabe Tenneson and his wife, Michella, live in Springfield, Missouri, where he attends Evangel University, completing a degree in art and biblical theology. Co-owner of Transformation Gallery & Tattoo, Gabe is a professional artist who has dedicated his life to blazing a trail within various subcultures and reclaiming the realms of fine art for the glorification of God. Privileged to represent Christ within the fine art and tattooing communities, Gabe feels honored to be part of the powerful and ordained Live Dead movement. He attributes all of his blessings, passions, and abilities to his Savior and Creator, who continues to transform his life.

Josh Tenneson lives in Springfield, Missouri, where he is working toward a degree in music industry and art at Evangel University. He is apprenticing under Gabe Tenneson and Austin Evans at Transformation Gallery & Tattoo, studying the art of tattooing and pursuing the fine arts of painting and graphic design. He has been blessed with opportunity after opportunity to learn and grow in the realms of life that he finds fulfillment in, and is humbled to be part of his Lord's vast plan.

Michael Buesking and his wife and two children live in Springfield, Missouri, where he is a member of the art faculty at Evangel University. Following his undergraduate art training at Southern Illinois University in Carbondale, Michael completed his master of fine arts degree in 2002 at the University of Missouri in Columbia. Michael joined Evangel's art department in 1991 to teach introductory and advanced oil painting, drawing, and art history. Now an associate professor at Evangel, Michael works to raise the profile of the visual arts in the body of Christ.

Prodigy Pixel's Jason Nill and Kelsey Davajon brought the Live Dead stories and artwork together, bringing this book to life. Prodigy Pixel is a Springfield, Missouri-based, award-winning graphic and web design agency founded in 2004 by two missionary kids with a knack for design and a passion for helping those who do good look good too. Prodigy has grown to provide more than 250 ministries, nonprofits, and missionaries with the tools they need to spread awareness, advocate for their causes, and tell their stories.

Special thanks to Omar Beiler for leadership to the Eurasia Region, Randy Bacon for his superb photography and cinematography efforts for Live Dead, Shannon Bacon for contributing thought-filled exercises and creative insight to this project, and Noor Barron and Shannon Varis for their beautiful photography used throughout this book.

TO ORDER ADDITIONAL COPIES OF THESE BOOKS PLEASE VISIT WWW.INFLUENCERESOURCES.COM.

LOOK FOR LIVE DEAD IRAN TO COME IN JUNE 2014.